D0059223

OTHER FIRESIDE BOOKS BY DANNY PEARY:

GUIDE FOR THE FILM FANATIC
CULT MOVIES 3
CLOSE-UPS: THE MOVIE STAR BOOK, *EDITOR*

H·O·W · T·O
BUY,
TRADE &
INVEST ·IN·
BASEBALL
CARDS
& COLLECTIBLES

·····SMART STRATEGIES
FOR STARTING, BUILDING & ENJOYING YOUR COLLECTION

BRUCE CHADWICK &
DANNY PEARY

A FIRESIDE BOOK
PUBLISHED BY SIMON & SCHUSTER INC.

NEW YORK   LONDON
SYDNEY   TORONTO
TOKYO

FIRESIDE

SIMON & SCHUSTER BUILDING
ROCKEFELLER CENTER
1230 AVENUE OF THE AMERICAS
NEW YORK, NEW YORK 10020

COPYRIGHT © 1989 BY BRUCE CHADWICK AND DANNY PEARY
ALL RIGHTS RESERVED
INCLUDING THE RIGHT OF REPRODUCTION
IN WHOLE OR IN PART IN ANY FORM.
FIRESIDE AND COLOPHON ARE REGISTERED TRADEMARKS
OF SIMON & SCHUSTER INC.

DESIGNED BY KATHY KIKKERT
MANUFACTURED IN THE UNITED STATES OF AMERICA

3 5 7 9 10 8 6 4 2

LIBRARY OF CONGRESS CATALOGING IN PUBLICATION DATA

CHADWICK, BRUCE.
HOW TO BUY, TRADE & INVEST IN BASEBALL CARDS & COLLECT-
IBLES : SMART STRATEGIES FOR STARTING, BUILDING & ENJOYING
YOUR COLLECTION / BRUCE CHADWICK & DANNY PEARY.
P.   CM.
"A FIRESIDE BOOK."

1. BASEBALL CARDS—COLLECTORS AND COLLECTING—UNITED
STATES.   2. BASEBALL—COLLECTIBLES—UNITED STATES.   3. BASE-
BALL—COLLECTIBLES—UNITED STATES—PRICES—UNITED STATES.
I. PEARY, DANNY.   II. TITLE.   III. TITLE: HOW TO BUY, TRADE, AND
INVEST IN BASEBALL CARDS AND COLLECTIBLES.
GV875.3.C45   1989
769'.49796357'0973075—DC20   89-6242
                                                                    CIP

ISBN: 0-671-67580-X

ACKNOWLEDGMENTS

This book would not have been possible without the help and encouragement of old and new friends. Our deepest gratitude goes to our editor, Jeff Neuman, and his assistant Hollie Manheimer, who made sure we weren't the only ones who understood what we were writing. We are also indebted to our agent, Chris Tomasino, the late Tim McGinnis, Sol Skolnick, and Sydny Weinberg-Miner for getting this project off the ground. A number of people at Simon and Schuster contributed to this work, but we would like to single out: Pat Eisemann, Liza Wright, Stephanie Bowling, Liz Cunning-

ACKNOWLEDGMENTS

ham, our designer Kathy Kikkert, our copy editor Steve Boldt, and our production editor George Turianski.

We would also like to thank—Dealers: Alan Rosen, Tony Craig, Dave Festberg, Colin Koeck, Joshua Evans, Nancy Batsell. Show promoters: Gloria Rothstein, Randy Thyberg, Harry Bryant, Jeff Schenker, Brian Sonnenberg, Harvey Brandwein and Steve Hisler, Dave Jurrist, Mike Grecco, Adam Newton, Richard Nader, and Ron Durham. Collectors: Henry Kurtz, Barry Halper, Jim Beckett, Bob Lemke, and Dan Albaugh. Manufacturers: Norman and Kenneth Liss (Topps), Anne Flavin (Score & Sportflic), and Neil Lewis (Donruss). Also: Bill Guilfoile (Baseball Hall of Fame), artists Bill Galo, Dick Perez, LeRoy Neiman, Andy Jurinko, and Bill Feldman. And Vic Ziegel, *Daily News* sports editor.

Special thanks to the players whose comments in interviews helped so much: Mickey Mantle, Whitey Ford, Ralph Terry, Harmon Killebrew, Lou Brock, Johnny Mize, Joe DiMaggio, Duke Snider, Moose Skowron, Jose Canseco, and Willie Mays.

Finally, we thank Margie, Suzanne, Rory and Zoë, quite a collection and our greatest investments.

TO MY WIFE, MARGIE, AND MY SON, RORY,
AND TO MY DAD,
WHO GAVE ME MY FIRST GLOVE

—BRUCE CHADWICK

TO SHIRLEY LOOPY AND CHIEF CALF CHILD

—DANNY PEARY

CONTENTS

H · O · W · T · O
BUY,
TRADE &
INVEST ·IN·
BASEBALL
CARDS
& COLLECTIBLES

INTRODUCTION

I started collecting baseball cards at the perfect time: it was the early fifties and I was young. In fact, even if it had been common knowledge that the inexpensive cards of the day would be worth a fortune thirty-five years later, I was too young to have cared. As it should be with all true card collectors, especially young kids, I collected cards for the sake of collecting cards; I didn't have anxiety attacks about whether a slight gum stain might lower a card from *mint* to *excellent* condition and reduce its resale value, or whether particular cards had investment potential, or whether it was a bad idea to trade a Yankee or Dodger star for a couple of favorite players on my lowly A's (I made the trade). Card collecting meant regular visits to candy and grocery stores, studying the wax packs on the counter and trying to guess which ones had the cards I needed to complete my sets, excitedly taking a couple of packs and putting down a handful of loose change (allowance money or a tiny donation from a kind relative), and quickly ripping open the wrapper, shoving the sweet-smelling gum into my mouth, and eagerly checking to see if I now owned one of the players I most coveted. What a great feeling it was to find new faces looking back at me. I was just as happy to get Smoky Burgess (as I did on my way to the dentist one memorable day of my youth) as an Ernie Banks rookie card, or an Angel Scull, Rufus Crawford, or Mickey Micelotta as a Mickey Mantle (not that I was ever foolish enough to trade my Mantles for Micelottas).

I regretted having helped my brother, who was five years older and quite a collector himself, paste his 1953 Topps set into an album and then trying to peel the cards off one by one, and having used a red crayon to draw mustaches on many Pirates and Cubs in that set (in which all players look about forty-five). However, I felt that baseball cards should be broken in, much like new gloves. I still believe worn cards have more character than mint cards. Today, the rule seems to be not to touch your cards once you acquire them in order to keep them in mint condition, but back in the fifties I couldn't go through a full summer's day without feverishly going through my card collection: letting my miserly hands run through the thousands of cards I kept in a box (later it would be two boxes), memorizing all the stats on the back of every card (my grammar school teachers never knew why I was such a whiz with numbers), and laying cards out according to teams and positions. I put rubber bands around them, took them out for trading sessions with young friends (although I think I was too obsessed with my cards to trade anything but doubles), and flipped my "dubs" toward the side of a building against a kid I hate to this day—I'm still convinced that all little boys with red hair and long fingernails cheat at card flipping (and marbles).

My brother and I eventually merged our card collections, only splitting them up each time we had a major fight. We had thousands of baseball cards (plus football, Davy Crockett, and most of every other card set that came out). My brother's baseball card purchases began in the late forties and ended around 1956 when, for reasons I couldn't fathom then, he suddenly lost interest. I put together nearly every complete set from 1954 through 1962 when—who would have suspected?—I mysteriously lost my interest in baseball cards, too . . . at the same time the Hardy Boys suddenly seemed too juvenile. I still loved my old cards, however, and moved them into my closet. Several years later, when I was about to follow my brother to college, I moved the boxes into the basement. Unfortunately, when my parents moved from New Jersey, they rented the house to many tenants. When my brother and I finally returned to the house in the mid-seventies to reclaim our collection, we made the sickening discovery that one of the tenants had walked off with almost all of our cards—cards that, even in their nonmint condition, were worth many thousands of dollars. No, my mother didn't throw out my cards, I tell everyone who asks, it was much worse.

Beginning in the mid-eighties, I attended card shows with the intention of reassembling my lost collection, particularly 1954 and 1955 Topps and Bowmans, the first cards I collected myself and still my favorite cards. (Yes, I know the 1955 Bowmans are mocked because the players are framed by color TV sets, but you have to remember how few of us had color sets at the time or had ever seen a baseball hero on a color set. These cards excited us.) The shows continue to amaze me. Everything is available, be it old cards or memorabilia (which I didn't collect in my youth) that you wouldn't think could possibly still exist. Even to someone not interested in collecting anything, these shows are fascinating.

But, there are problems. I get annoyed with dealers who know nothing about baseball history pitching their "beautiful"—the most common word at shows—cards, and sounding like sly tailors who try to sell you an ugly, ill-fitting suit. I'm upset that many of the young kids who attend the shows have become young capitalists, only interested in buying "investment quality" cards and autographed items that they can later sell at higher prices. It's fine to put together a collection that has value, but card and memorabilia collecting should be fun, not a business enterprise. Also, I'm upset that star players of past and present accept money from promoters to sell their autographs (especially to kids). Yes, I realize that the players don't want to be exploited by dealers, fake admirers (who know nothing of their careers), and kids who make a profit by selling their autographs. But is nothing sacred? And I'm truly shocked at the high prices being charged for cards that I bought in my youth a penny at a time. It's particularly irritating that the high prices are not the result of those star cards being any more rare than common cards—they aren't—but because dealers are buying and keeping the star cards in short supply so their prices will rise. I know I will have to pay an inordinate amount of money if I want to buy cards of the best players of the fifties. Fortunately, I don't prefer stars over commons, and I don't care if a star card is worn—I'm looking to keep these cards, not resell them, and besides, my missing cards were worn, too. So, like many of you, I am slowly but surely replacing my lost cards with inexpensive, far-from-mint cards, which can be found if one looks hard enough. And I am having a great time.

I have lost most of my cynicism about the world of card and memorabilia collecting, eighties-style. Once you know the rules and the good-guy collectors and yes, good-guy dealers in the card business, it can be quite enjoyable to take part. There's actually a sense of triumph if you make a good deal: what a pleasure it is to buy something you love and then discover someone trying to sell the identical item at an exorbitant price. It's exciting to put together a collection, even if such a collection in better condition would be worth several times more money. And it's a rewarding challenge to figure out unusual and interesting items to collect. Nevertheless, there are few worse things than getting gypped, making the wrong purchase, or passing on an item you later learn will eventually become much more valuable.

With too many card sets on the market and so much merchandise available, with various dealers hawking the same cards and memorabilia at different prices, with everything being publicized as a collectible and being termed "a sound investment," the word of the day is definitely "confusion." I decided that what collectors need to end that confusion is a book that will help us make decisions regarding purchases and trades of baseball cards and baseball collectibles. Collectors need to know what they should buy, where they can find it, and from whom they should buy it. I wanted to come up with a book that would help collectors relax and not worry that they have "blown it" if they don't buy every card set and every collectible put out on the already terribly saturated market. I wanted a book that would help collectors devise a strategy to prevent them from making big mistakes and also to help them assemble collections that are both valuable and personally enjoyable for the least amount of money.

Because I am, deliberately, an outsider to the card and collectible world, and someone who knows the right questions but not all the answers, I sought a coauthor who is an expert on the subject but no dealer himself and someone not interested in making a profit in the baseball card and collectibles boom. I recruited Bruce Chadwick, who writes a popular column on baseball cards called The Card Shop for the New York *Daily News*. As is the case for many adults who have become card and memorabilia collectors, Bruce immersed himself in the hobby (he prefers memorabilia to card collecting) when he realized it was a rare hobby he could share with his young son. For this book, Bruce would answer my questions and help me devise a smart game plan for card and memorabilia collectors.

Our goal is not to make you rich, but to help you prudently and economically put together a collection that is both personally satisfying and valuable.

—DANNY PEARY

When Danny Peary first met me, he was expecting a longtime baseball fanatic, a man who could tell him the starting lineup of the Chicago White Sox in 1925, a man who had Joe DiMaggio's slugging percentage at the tip of his tongue, a man who had been collecting baseball cards since the day Abner Doubleday got tired of soccer. What he got was a very unusual fan and a very unusual collector.

I was indeed a great baseball fan. My dad used to take me to Yankee Stadium all the time. I would sit there and praise the great Mickey Mantle, while my father would snort and tell me that he was good but certainly couldn't hold the Babe's bat. I played Little League baseball (very badly) but right around the age of thirteen stopped playing and stopped going to games. I had lots of cards but had just discovered girls (though they didn't discover me until many years later). Baseball and cards ended abruptly. In fact, I didn't see another baseball game, live or on television, until twenty-one years later.

That spring, my six-year-old son signed up for Little League. I brought him to the opening day parade and walked down to a large group of people to introduce him to whoever his manager would be. A large, burly man saw me walking and said, indicating my son, "Yours?" I nodded.

"Congratulations. You're the team's manager. Here's your roster, here's your equipment bag [dropped on my foot], and here's a hat for you [too small]. Get them in line, tell them to be quiet, and have a good season," he said.

So began a career of Little League managing that spanned four years (24 and 24, not bad). At the age of thirty-four, I fell completely in love with the game of baseball all over again. Bart Giamatti once told me that people live and die and the tide of history ebbs and flows, but baseball goes on forever. He's right. Whether it's seven-year-old kids running to third instead of first or Don Mattingly hitting one into heaven at the Stadium, baseball goes on forever.

In the spring of 1986, I bought my son his first pack of baseball cards. The next day he came home elated—he had just traded one of his cards and gotten fifty in return. Turns out, the one was a $10 Dwight Gooden rookie card and the fifty were worth 2¢ each. That got the sports fan and businessman in him interested, and he and I started collecting. We've been doing it ever since. The huge baseball card collecting market prompted me to suggest to my newspaper, the New York *Daily News*, that they let me write a baseball card column. That was over a year ago, and it has been a great success. It seems all of America collects cards and memorabilia (or wants to).

Then Danny Peary came to me with this idea—a book that would help people buy the right cards and avoid the wrong ones, build a collection that they can enjoy, and one that might, in time, amount to some money.

This book is about how people can do that, based on the way my son and I did just that. Oh, ours is a very small collection and not worth very much, but it's great fun, and every night we look at our autographed baseballs, photos, signed bats, and stacks and stacks of cards. My son's thirteen now and we spend hours each week going to card shops and shows. It's wonderful time together for us—and for all fathers and sons in collecting. But at thirteen, it's probably his time to discover girls this summer. That's okay, as long as she's a Yankee or Mets fan.

Every night, after my son goes to sleep and my wife is nodding off, I look through our little collection in the converted playroom downstairs. I close my eyes hard and think back to when I was a kid collecting baseball cards—all those beautiful '57 through '61 cards—and I transport myself back to when I was a kid. My dad is alive again and smiling that big toothy smile, the two of us are in a car on our way to Yankee Stadium—getting ready to run under the subway el, wolf down some hot dogs, buy a program, and sit down in seats NOT behind a column and watch Mickey Mantle and Roger Maris tear apart the Orioles. It's the summer of 1961 and all is right with the world.

—BRUCE CHADWICK

THE BASICS

CHAPTER 1

GETTING STARTED

We realize that you are anxious to begin buying baseball cards and collectibles. However, it will be to your benefit to be patient. It is essential to learn as much as you can about the card and collectible market before jumping in.

An obvious warning: Do not go out and start buying cards and memorabilia before you learn what is available and what you should be paying for it. We certainly don't want to discourage you from acquiring a particular item that strikes your fancy simply because it may not have investment potential—we applaud such purchases—but too many anxious collectors, especially novices, lay down their money before they realize that (1) they can get the same item elsewhere for a lower price, and (2) there is probably another item on which they'd rather spend their money if they knew it existed.

ESSENTIAL BROWSING

If you haven't done so already, go to your local card stores and browse around; become familiar with what cards and collectibles are readily available and what prices are being charged. If a proprietor becomes annoyed with your questions and your leaving with nothing but his catalogue, seek out another dealer, one who remembers that card and memorabilia collecting is still a hobby to most of us.

Go to a couple of card shows; preferably a small one with fifty tables or fewer and, if the promoter could get him, a Mario Mendoza-type signing autographs, and a large one with over one hundred tables, dealers from several states, and star players signing autographs. Get your autographs (or for now, just watch the autographing process) and then walk up and down the aisles. You will see cards from every decade displayed on the dealer tables. (The smaller shows tend to have newer cards because kids make up a large percentage of those in attendance.) Here, more than in card stores, you will also discover a wealth of baseball memorabilia. Take a look at the prices of the old cards and prize collectibles. Have your initial shock. Yes, many prices are steep, even outrageous. But for no discernible reason, others are low. You must understand that we're discussing a hobby so weird that Topps 1956 checklists are valued more than the cards of Ted Williams, Sandy Koufax, Roberto Clemente, Willie Mays, Hank Aaron, and every other player but Mickey Mantle; and that

Mantle cards and memorabilia are worth more than identical items of any other player in history, although no one claims he was the greatest player. So look at the dealer tables, shake your head, and begin to think about what you eventually hope to include in your collection and what you will have to leave for more obsessed and richer collectors.

Check out the souvenir stand the next time you go to a major or minor league ballpark. Pay no attention to the balloon bats, whoopee cushions, and other junk, but see if there are more interesting collectibles that you might like to own eventually: special-issue baseball cards, the deservedly popular Surf (laundry detergent) books of the home team (featuring photos of Topps cards of the team's players dating back to 1952), posters, pins, patches. Note how much they cost so you can compare the ballpark prices to card show and dealer prices for the same material. Pick up a schedule, and if you are planning to attend more games, get tickets to the best promotion and giveaway nights so you can walk away with free collectibles.

If you are passing a collectibles or antique store, go in and browse. See if these stores carry any baseball memorabilia. You may find some unusual items. If you don't see anything, ask. You are under no obligation to buy anything.

In later sections of this book, we will tell you what to buy and what not to buy at card stores, card shows, souvenir stands, collectibles shops, antique stores, and other card and collectibles outlets.

HELPFUL PUBLICATIONS

It's surprising how many people who attend card shows and visit card shops aren't aware that there are price guides and hobby magazines, newsletters and newspapers, that will help them make wise purchases, track down those special items they are looking for, and understand the hobby much better. Indeed, you can find most of these publications being sold by dealers at the card shows and shops, or you can order them through the mail. We recommend that all card collectors pick up one of two annual price guides: *The Sports Collectors Digest Baseball Card Price Guide,* compiled by Bob Lemke (editor of *Sports Collectors Digest*) and Dan Albaugh, and *The Sport Americana Baseball Card Price Guide,* by Dr. James Beckett and Dennis W. Eckes. You will find more than 70,000 cards listed in each of these thick paperbacks. All the major issue sets are listed in each volume, plus all the most popular specialty sets. It's fascinating just to flip pages in these books and see the volume and diversity of cards in existence—you're bound to feel waves of nostalgia when you come across cards you had way back when. Can you afford to buy them today in mint condition, in which they have their strongest investment potential? How about in a less expensive nonmint condition?

Both books give several prices for each listed card, so you will know what you should pay if you find new and old cards in mint or such lesser conditions as near-mint, excellent-mint, excellent, very good, good, fair, and poor. Dealers in card shops and at card shows, who want to give you a "fair" price rather than a bargain, almost always use these books to price the cards they are selling. You'll find that when a dealer temporarily leaves his table at a card show, whoever watches his wares uses one of these books to price unmarked cards so the dealer won't be upset at transactions made in his or her absence.

When you attempt to buy a particular card, you'll discover that the book price for top-condition individual cards is pretty much adhered to by dealers—although they will offer top-condition full sets at prices higher than listed in either book. However, be warned that dealers usually ignore the lower prices in these books and charge more for their poor, fair, good, very good, excellent and near-mint cards. Often, they will make up a designation of their own, like fair-good or excellent-plus, to rationalize why they are charging more than the book price for a card. Of course, if you tried to sell the exact card to them, they'd insist it is excellent-minus. It is a fact in the baseball card world: whoever owns the card assumes it is in better condition than it really is.

All collectors *must* remember that the book prices represent what dealers charge customers and are about 40 percent higher (more in many cases) than what customers will get from dealers for the same cards. Also remember that while dealers smooth-talk customers into buying cards in less than mint condition by saying they have high investment potential, you would have a nearly impossible time trying to sell such cards to dealers because of their *low* investment potential. So if you buy a card that is less than excellent—especially a post-1970 card—understand that you may be stuck with it because a dealer will pay you a lot less than it cost you.

Beckett also issues a small annual called *The Official Price Guide to Baseball Cards*. This national best-seller contains listings of the major issue sets and several specialty sets (Kellogg's, Hostess). It's great to carry around at shows because it fits into your pocket. Since the prices are out of date almost as soon as the book hits the stores, we recommend that you use the book like a checklist: check off the cards you have in each set, and then, when you come across cards from particular sets you're interested in, it's easy to open this book to see which cards you already have and which cards are missing. You may think everyone should know what cards they own, but it becomes confusing because you see some cards so often you forget you don't own them; also, if you collected in your youth, you may not recall if you own a particular card today or owned it back then.

If you're interested in easily tracking down cards for particular players—every collector should have the cards of his/her favorite player!—you may want to get hold of Beckett's *The Sport Americana Baseball Card Alphabetical Checklist.* Every player who has appeared on a baseball card is listed, in alphabetical order. Every card he has appeared on, even group shots, is listed under his name, year by year.

Beckett has also edited a book that will be of interest to those not interested in cards. His *The Sport Americana Baseball Collectibles Price Guide* gives the market value of bread labels, coins and discs, decals, fabric items (blankets, felt pennants, silks), lids and caps, pins, stamps, stickers, tattoos, flip movies, posters, transfers, rub-offs, paper inserts, etc. There are many kinds of collectibles you won't find listed in the Beckett book, so you may also want to look at John Carpentier's pamphlet, *JC's Baseball Collectibles Price Guide,* which gives general price ranges for tickets, cards, jerseys, yearbooks, statues, sheet music, schedules, programs, scorecards, postcards, photographs, pennants, jewelry, guides, annuals, magazines, toys, games, press pins, and press passes. The new quarterly *Legends* updates prices on limited edition items, including porcelain plates, lithographs, posters, figurines, mugs, and bats.

Autograph collectors will find *The Sport Americana Baseball Address List* indispensable. This small reference guide by R. J. "Jack" Smalling and Dennis W. Eckes includes mailing addresses for all living current and former major leaguers. But we hesitate to recommend this well-researched book only because many players consider autograph-seekers who write them at home a terrible nuisance. Many players refuse to answer autograph requests, and others do so reluctantly (some charge fees) and take up to a year to respond, because they suspect their autographs will be sold by the person who contacted them. If you want an autograph for *your* collection, say this in your letter. Also let the player know that you want his autograph because you are aware of what he did in his career. To show that you aren't out to sell his autograph, request a personalized autograph; and if you want to impress upon him that you aren't out to make a profit, send him a baseball card to sign—he will know that, ridiculously, the value of most cards decreases when autographed. Don't send too many items or too many of the same item to be autographed—this will make him suspicious that you plan to sell them. Send thank-you notes when you receive an autograph, assuring the player that you're no wheeler-dealer. Enclose a self-addressed, stamped envelope or a self-addressed package with sufficient return postage.

Not long ago, the annual price guides were enough to get collectors from one year to the next. But now, investors are so anxious about the fluctuating values of their latest purchases that monthly price guides have come on the market. These are also used as price references at card shops and shows. If you think price updates are necessary, try *Beckett's Baseball Card Monthly,* published by Statabase Inc., and *Baseball Cards,* published by Krause Publications, to see if either fits your needs. (For those of you who are part of the minor league card craze, there is *Mary Huston's Monthly Minor League Price Guide*.) Because monthly price changes are quite small and are also recorded by the hobby newspapers, we suggest that you subscribe to these magazines only if you enjoy the articles and letter sections, which mostly feature inquiries from readers about the value of cards (especially error and variation cards) and memorabilia they have found. Readers also write in to gripe about sneaky dealers and rude players at autograph sessions—those letters are fun to read.

Perhaps more valuable to the average collector than any of the aforementioned books and magazines are the hobby journals. All contain many dealer ads, auction ads, reader ads, card show information, price updates for major-issue sets, discussions of new sets and products on the market, reader feedback, and articles about the hobby. The most enterprising also include interviews with or essays about former, present, and future major leaguers. Of the hobby newspapers, we recommend first the weekly *Sports Collectors Digest;* it has an excellent staff of writers, includes interesting interviews, and is truly at the vanguard of the hobby. Ironically, many card dealers and coin stores place ads in this newspaper with prices for individual cards and sets that *far* exceed the prices listed in *SCD*'s weekly roundup. Also highly recommended are the other major hobby newspapers, *Baseball Card News, Baseball Hobby News,* Lew Lipset's compact *Old Judge*—which deals with old cards dating back to the nineteenth century—and *Tuff Stuff,* which is ideal for collectors interested in rookie cards and minor league sets.

WHAT DO YOU HAVE ALREADY?

As you visit card shops, attend card shows, and read the literature on the hobby, you should be trying to decide what you want to collect. But before you make your final decision, *figure out what you already own.* If you haven't done so, take an inventory of your own collection. We realize many of you are reluctant to call yourselves baseball card or memorabilia collectors, but from now on try thinking about all the baseball material you have as a *collection.* Your ragged magazines, miscellaneous cards, tickets, and odds and ends will suddenly seem to have value once you bring them all together and catalogue them. So empty your trunks, shoe boxes, drawers, and closet shelves. Set aside a nice area for your budding collection. Group your magazines, yearbooks, scorecards, stubs, and cards (take off those damaging rubber bands!). Organize your collection. Mark down the condition of your memorabilia, magazines, and cards.

According to *Sports Collectors Digest,* card conditions are as follows:

MINT: A perfect card. Well-centered with all corners sharp and square. No creases, stains, edge nicks, surface marks, yellowing or fading, regardless of age.

NEAR-MINT: A nearly perfect card. May have one corner not perfectly sharp. May be slightly off-center. No surface marks, creases, or loss of gloss.

EXCELLENT: Corners are still fairly sharp with only moderate wear. Borders may be off-center. No creases or stains on fronts or backs, but may show slight loss of surface luster.

VERY GOOD: Shows obvious handling. May have rounded corners, minor creases, moderate gum or wax stains. No major creases, tape marks, writing, etc.

GOOD: A well-worn card, but exhibits no intentional damage. May have major or multiple creases. Corners may be rounded well beyond card border.

FAIR: A complete card, but contains damage such as writing on card back, tack holes, and heavy creases.

(Take note that Dr. Beckett's publications have slightly different but equally valid condition classifications. Beckett's worst classification is "Poor," for abused cards.)

Look at your collection and see if you have anything to build on. If you held on to the yearbooks of your favorite team for six of the last ten years, you might consider trying to find the missing years. Perhaps you have ticket stubs from several major league parks—maybe you want to have stubs from all the parks. Or scorecards? Perhaps you have autographs from several players who were on a particular team in, say, 1975—maybe you want to get autographs from other players on that team. If you have many cards from a particular set, consider filling out that set, especially if there aren't many cards in that set (as was the case with the Bowman sets of 1948–55 and the early Topps sets) and you are lucky enough to have the highest-priced cards from that set. (Check our set charts at the end of the second section of this book to see how many cards are in each set, the number of low-priced commons you will have to buy, and the number and prices of high-price cards.)

Memorabilia collectors couldn't make a wiser decision than to seek out collectibles relating to star players (dead or alive); card collectors couldn't make a sounder investment than purchasing complete sets. But since your goal is not necessarily to make the most money but to put together a collection that will both give you pleasure and be a solid investment, you have numerous choices about what and whom to collect. Try giving your collection a theme. The possibilities are limitless; here are just a few suggestions:

1. *The first black on each major league franchise*
2. *Black pitchers*
3. *Cuban players*
4. *One-year major leaguers*
5. *Bad players*
6. *Cult players*
7. *Players with alliterative names*
8. *Flops*
9. *A player's final season (rather than his rookie year)*
10. *Mets third basemen*
11. *Players on new franchises*
12. *Players on final rosters of franchises that will move*
13. *Players with zany names*
14. *Notoriously bad fielders*
15. *Dominican players*
16. *Latin players*
17. *Players born in Europe*
18. *Jewish players*
19. *Players who died or were killed during their careers*
20. *Catchers*
21. *Players who had drug or alcohol problems*
22. *Players from certain states*
23. *Double-play combinations*
24. *Players who had fights with each other*
25. *All-Star starters from a particular year*
26. *Players who became managers*

27. *MVP players*
28. *Players traded from a particular team*
29. *Unheralded stars*
30. *Future Hall of Famers*
31. *Hall of Famers*
32. *Center fielders*
33. *Players who were both Mets and Yankees*
34. *Players who were both Giants and Dodgers*
35. *Players who were both Cubs and White Sox*
36. *Players who were traded for each other*
37. *Italian players*
38. *Forgettable and forgotten players*
39. *Players who homered in their first at-bats*
40. *Players who never homered*
41. *Players on particular teams*
42. *Cy Young winners*
43. *Homer champions*
44. *Rookies of the Year*
45. *Ugly players*
46. *Players who went by their nicknames or middle names*
47. *Strikeout champions*
48. *Minor league stars*
49. *Batting champions*
50. *College graduates*
51. *Negro League players*
52. *Players under 5'9" and over 6'3"*
53. *Players who became broadcasters*

When cataloguing your own collection, make up a "Want List." When you learn more about pricing, mark down the highest price you are willing to pay for cards and memorabilia on this list. Also make a list of cards (including doubles) and memorabilia that you don't care if you keep. Whatever you find dispensable in your collection, someone out there will gladly take off your hands in the right deal. Perhaps you have no attachment to certain collectibles you have—you may have forgotten you had them anyway. Or perhaps you have only a handful of cards from a particular year and would just as soon trade them for cards of a year you are collecting. If in that handful of cards you, for some reason, have one of the most valuable cards of a particular year, you can elect to trade that one card—if it is worth $20 or more—for an entire set of cards, or several sets of cards.

THE SAFE INITIAL PURCHASE

While you are pondering what to collect, make a minimal purchase to satisfy your "need to buy something *now*." There is one purchase you can make without knowing anything about the hobby business, and that you won't regret later. *We recommend that all collectors, even those much more interested in collectibles than cards, begin each year by acquiring the newest set of Topps cards.* Baseball cards are still the best way to learn about the stars and nonstars of the game, and the annual Topps set is guaranteed to be attractive, informative, and a solid investment. If you can splurge, also buy the other major-issue sets—the attractive Donruss, the hardest-to-find Fleer, Score (with the best card-backs in card history), and the new, expensive Upper Deck. Each of these sets compares favorably to Topps in quality and in rare years may feature a prized rookie (Don Mattingly in 1984, Jose Canseco in 1986, Gregg Jefferies in 1988) that will make it more valuable than the same year's Topps set, which lacks that rookie. Still, if you buy one set, make it Topps. The IBM of card sets, only Topps has the long tradition, current financial success, and a guaranteed bright future to make its annual sets a sure bet. Any player who makes it to the big leagues will eventually have his Topps debut, and his first Topps card will be valuable when he becomes a star (although perhaps not as valuable as his first card in the year-earlier sets of the competitors). It is almost a certainty that at least one new player in each Topps set will eventually make it big in the big leagues—his success will cause his rookie card and the entire set that includes it to increase in value. We have seen that every year; all past Topps sets—even those without a rookie who becomes a superstar—have increased in value. There's little doubt that this trend will continue, so it's comforting to know you have each set, and have bought them at their lowest prices.

All the card stores in your area stock Topps sets, including the factory-collated sets that, if the box remains sealed, have the best investment value. (But we don't recommend that a hobbyist buy only one set during the year and *never* look at the cards. Do that and you're a broker, not a collector. This is supposed to be *fun*.) Card shops may not give you the best deal on the latest set, but they're the best place to go if you are in a hurry to get it. You can probably get a slightly lower price from dealers at the next local card show, but you have to pay an admission price to get in. If you don't mind waiting a month or two for delivery, you may want to order from a dealer who advertises in a hobby magazine or *The Sporting News* early in the year, before the cards are available to the public. Remember to factor in postage; in fact, the best deals on new card sets often come from dealers who pay postage themselves to make it easier on prospective new customers. The best deal on new Topps sets (and the other sets as well) often comes from a small dealer who is trying to lure customers away from the bigger, better-known dealers. It's not a bad idea to order your new set from a smaller dealer, but don't automatically assume that since he is giving you the best deal on the new set he is also giving the best deals on earlier sets that are also priced in the ad. If you're going to make several purchases, also compare set prices for those other years.

Of course many collectors, particularly youngsters, don't have the $18–20 at any one time that is necessary to buy a Topps set. Instead, they will be forced to spend much more than the cost of a boxed set over the course of a year, buying wax and cello packs and trying to put together a set. If you are such a collector, or someone who has bought a sealed set and still enjoys putting together whole sets with candy store purchases (as we all did in the good old days), use all those doubles and triples you will accumulate to deal for missing cards. Card shop owners and most dealers at card shows will buy your star card doubles (at about 60 percent guide prices); use the money you get from them to buy more cards in stores. If you are trading your star-card doubles to another collector, remember that this card is *not* a double to the other guy, but the only one he'll have in his set. So get fair value. Because you will have to do a lot of trading if you want to put together a set piecemeal without spending too much money trying to get the final elusive cards, it is definitely wise to become partners with a few friends. Agree on a sum of money you will each spend on cards. Then, each time one of you gets a double, give that card to someone in the group who doesn't have that particular card; he'll later have to return the favor. Expect major arguments, but you'll enjoy the camaraderie.

CHAPTER 2

BUYING BASEBALL CARDS

Baseball-card collecting used to be so simple. You tried to get as many cards as you could from the newest set by buying them at the corner candy store, trading your doubles, and flipping against your friends. Other than cards of your favorite player or players on your favorite team, and a couple of elusive cards you needed to complete your set, all cards had about the same value to you. Today, collecting cards is much different. You want to accumulate the most valuable cards in each set, and you want to keep your new cards in mint condition—something you never worried about before. When you open a pack of cards, you'll find yourself zipping through the common players in search of stars and rookies. Cards of common players are valued at just 3¢ and are readily available at shows and shops. But star cards can go for three or four times the price of the pack you bought and will increase in value each year.

Even more in demand are rookie cards—if you get them, hold on to them, even if you never heard of the player. Some rookie cards are valued at 3¢ if nothing much is expected of the players—even so, if they hit it big, your card will zoom in price. Cards of "rated rookies," players who are expected by the experts to have solid careers, are usually worth about 25¢, with a good chance to shoot up if the player starts out well. The most promising and publicized rookies, especially those who play for spotlight teams in New York or Los Angeles, often have cards valued at several dollars *even before they play their first games in the big leagues!* These coveted cards may be the most expensive cards in the set, and they will go up if the player becomes a star. Remember that the rookie card of every player will remain his most valued card.

Buying baseball cards also used to be simple. You just went to your corner candy store, plopped down your penny, nickel, or dime, and got packs of cards containing one, five, or ten players. But now that cards are considered a great investment, every collector, including kids, wants to purchase cards in the most economical way. This means that collectors must determine their particular budgets and then decide whether to buy cards in packs, boxes, cases, lots, or sets, whether to buy valued mint cards or nonmint cards they may never be able to sell, and whether to buy old or new cards, rookies or proven stars, white and/or black players. Fortunately, there are advantages to every type of card collecting.

WAX PACKS AND CELLO PACKS

Every true card collector—even those who buy sets or in bulk—should continue the fine tradition of buying cards at the local candy store. Most candy stores carry Topps wax packs (with bubble gum that doesn't taste as good as it used to) and many carry Topps cello(phane) packs. If you do a little searching, you can also find stores that sell Donruss, Score, and Upper Deck. You'll have to find Fleer at the card shop.

Save your money so you can buy several wax packs at the same time, all coming from the same box on the counter. One box of 36 wax packs contains almost half a set, so if you buy, say, half a box of wax packs, you have a better chance of getting more star cards and less duplicates than if you buy one or two packs at a time from different boxes. Watch out for "cherry picking"—someone opening packs, removing the stars, and replacing them with common cards, then resealing the packs. If you buy a lot of packs from one store and consistently find few stars, then there is good reason to stop buying your cards there, because Topps contends that it produces the same number of cards for every player. This situation doesn't happen often, but last year we purchased 40 packs of cards from one New York candy store without getting a Darryl Strawberry, Don Mattingly, Dwight Gooden, Dave Winfield, Gary Carter, Keith Hernandez, Mark McGwire, or Jose Canseco. It may have been bad luck, but if this happens to you, definitely change stores. Or change strategy: we bought ten packs from a previously *unopened* box in that store and immediately got half of the above players.

Investors will find a real benefit in buying many wax packs at once. Buy 18 packs. If you discover the expensive cards you wanted in the first nine or ten packs, keep the other packs sealed. Unopened packs have tremendous investment potential. A forty-cent Topps 1985 pack is worth $3.50–4.00 today, having gone up ten times in value! Even a 1987 Donruss pack, for which there was never a demand or a scarcity, has climbed to more than $1.25 in two years. Topps packs from 1975 are going for $20 each. Go back to the 1954 Bowmans; the set is now worth $2600. An unopened pack sells for $400, although few combinations of five cards from that set equal or surpass $400 in value. So keep those unopened packs.

Should you buy unopened wax packs from previous years? If the price is fair, if there are a number of players in those sets that have high prices, and if you can afford a number of packs so your chances of getting the really high-priced players improves dramatically, yes. The more money you have to spend, the better chance you have to get the one or two high-valued cards that will more than cover your investment. Ideally, buy several packs, open a few and discover a few star players, and keep the rest of the packs unopened for future sale. You definitely will be able to sell these unopened packs in a couple years for more than your purchase price, especially if you bought in quantity and got the dealer to lower his per-pack price.

Unopened cello packs are also good investments. The ones that are really coveted are those in which a high-priced card is one of the three visible cards on top or three cards on the bottom whose backs can be seen. Snap those up because *the one card is worth more than what you pay for the pack!* You can open the pack and add the valuable card to your collection, then see if there are other cards of value inside that will make your purchase an even bigger steal. But if you don't need that card, keep the pack sealed for possible resale in the future—the pack will go up considerably even if a star card isn't visible, so the card's presence will definitely make it go up even more. Many wise (and incredibly meticulous) collectors prefer cello packs to wax packs because they can look at the cards on top and the numbers of the cards on the bottom, and since Topps cuts its card sheets the same way each time, they can figure out which cards are hidden inside. Since they can determine which, if any, star cards are inside, they can select which cello packs to buy and which to leave on the store counter. If you want to, study card numbers and see if the pattern-system holds true. If it works, fine; if it doesn't, figure that Topps has decided to thwart such sneakiness.

BOXES

If you have the money to buy in slightly larger quantities, buy boxes of cards. However, don't buy them at corner candy stores or department stores. There you'd get 36 packs of Topps cards for $14.40, exactly what you'd pay if you bought each pack individually for 40¢. Buy boxes at card shows, where the dealer can sell them to you for $11 or $12 because he gets them for $9 each wholesale. You can get great bargains on all years. For instance, if today you wanted to buy 36 packs of the highly valued Topps 1985 set, you'd pay $3.50 each if you bought them one pack at a time, for a total of $126; if you buy a box, you will pay less than $90. In a box you get 500 cards for at least 30 percent less than you'd pay for the same number of cards in individual packs, so if you buy six boxes, you'll actually be getting the sixth box free.

What if you wanted to turn around and sell that extra box of cards to get enough money to make other card purchases? You must remember that because dealers buy in quantity at discount prices, they can afford to sell in quantity at less than price-guide prices. They deal in such high volume that it is easier to sell the box than to sell the individual packs within the boxes. This practice doesn't apply to you when you want to sell your single box of cards. To maximize your profits, open the box and sell the unopened wax packs at the individual pack rate.

Buying a box of new cards for $11 or $12 is a bargain because you're very likely to get 11 or 12 cards that are worth $1 each, plus numerous 50¢ cards. You could double your money. The worst thing that can happen is that you acquire only a few star cards. If that prospect worries you, and you have more money to cover yourself, buy 3 boxes for $33–36 and you'll be able to put together at least one set, with all the stars included. That set alone will be worth $30 in two years, and you will also have many other cards, including star doubles and triples, to trade, sell, or help you begin a second set. Many kids pack up 100 mixed cards—stars and commons—and sell them to friends for $4–5.

CASES

You can buy a case of twenty-four 1989 Topps boxes, containing 12,000 cards, for about $169. That's 1.4¢ per card. A case saves you nearly 50 percent in bulk, a great deal. Also, cases appreciate wildly. A Topps case that went for $159 in 1985 sells for nearly $1,000 today. The smart thing to do is to buy one case a year and store it away. After about five years, sell the oldest case for a tremendous profit, which you will reinvest in the hobby; do the same every year after that. This way you will never have more than five cases on hand, so you can still feel like a collector rather than a dealer.

LOTS

You will see many dealer ads in hobby magazines offering lots for sale. For the uninitiated, a lot is a group of, say, 50 to 100 similar cards: 100 Topps 1989 Cansecos, 50 Score 1987 Boggs, 100 VG-condition Yankees from fifties and sixties Topps sets, 50 Excellent-condition cards from 1953 Topps, 100 cards from 1984 Donruss, 100 common-player cards from 1958–65 Topps, 50 mint rookie cards from 1986 Fleer, etc. If a player, card year, and card condition aren't specified, dealers reserve the right to send cards of their choice. Lots are geared toward (1) collectors who want either cards of their favorite team or to put together starter collections; and (2) speculators who buy cards of individual stars and promising rookies at bargain high-quantity rates with the intention of selling them off one at a time if the player's performance increases the value of the card.

Lots can be good buys because the dealer is willing to give good prices when he sells in quantity. You usually save 20–30 percent on lots. You can buy 100 Topps 1986 Rickey Henderson cards for $10, 100 Topps 1988 Wade Boggs cards for $35, 100 Topps 1958 Excellent-condition cards for $100, 50 Topps 1955 VG-Ex-condition cards for $110. However, if you buy 100 cards of a promising rookie for 20¢ each, and he flops, you won't even be able to sell his cards at 3¢. (Fortunately, you won't have invested very much in his card if you bought a lot.) You'll even have difficulty selling your numerous cards of a star who suddenly fades.

Hobbyists who want to put together starting collections should be careful about ordering 100-card lots. First of all, order from an established dealer, not another collector who puts an ad in a hobby magazine, because there's no telling if that other collector will properly grade the cards he is sending you. His idea of near-mint or very good condition may greatly differ from your own. Also, don't be excited by a lot with 100 cards from a five- to ten-year period. You can end up with ten common players from ten different years—lousy starter sets. Even getting 100 common and semistar cards from one year isn't such a great deal if there are over 660 cards in a set. It's better to save your money if buying the 100 cards won't make it any easier to put together a set—know that there are few times that 100 cards, 200, 300, 400, or even 500 common cards will help you put together a set at less expense than you'd have if you simply bought the set whole. One extraordinary fact should be kept in mind at all times: *the combined price of the star cards in each set is often more than the book price of an entire set.* That makes the common cards essentially worthless—something to consider if you have the urge to buy commons by lot. The only time it is smart to buy commons by lot is when you have already acquired the star cards from the particular set. Then it's nice to know that common cards are available and inexpensive.

SETS

Sets are the best buys you can make. A new 792-card Topps set or 660-card Score set can be purchased today for around $20, less at shows, and may go up in value by 25 percent or more per year. The 1987 Topps set, loaded with good rookie cards, originally sold at $18 at card shows. Today it's worth $28. The 1985 set sold at $17 and at this writing is worth $90. The 1971 set sold for $12 and is today worth $1,000.

Why are sets so valuable? Cards get lost—sets don't. You

buy a set in a box and keep it together; cards wind up all over the place. If you display a set in plastic sheets, you tend to keep it in one binder. Cards in plastic sheets wind up scattered among teams, hitters, pitchers, etc. Sets remain a unit.

Significantly, sets are easy to resell to dealers, while most individual cards are not. A dealer will pay you only $5 for a $10 card, but he will pay you $30 for a $35 or $40 set. That's because he can buy sets in bulk and pluck out star cards for resale. He can buy a 1967 set and pull out a $400 Tom Seaver and still have hundreds of other valuable cards. Or he can buy your 1987 set that retails at $29 for $24 or so and sit on it for five years and resell it for $100. So can you.

Sets are also rare, especially pre-1970 sets. Individual cards float around, sold or traded from one dealer to another. A person puts together a set and keeps it—or buys a set and stores it. They are bought and put away. They're gone. Some never surface again. Their rarity makes them a great investment for future resale, even in nonmint condition.

Also, in a set you know you have one of each card, leaving you free to buy and sell and trade duplicate star cards you find at a store. No matter what happens, you always have your Mattingly or Canseco back home in the set.

MINT CARDS: BEST FOR INVESTORS

Condition is extremely important in card collecting. A card worth $100 in mint condition is likely to be valued at $40–60 in very good–excellent condition and $10–15 in fair-good condition. More important to the investor: mint cards not only have a much higher price increase from year to year than lesser-condition cards, but also have a much higher rate of increase. Over five-year, ten-year, or longer periods of time, both the mint card's price increase and price rate increase are substantially higher than those of lesser-condition cards. If you collect lesser-condition cards, you can certainly buy them cheaper, but you will have to sell them cheaper. Only mint cards can be sold at top prices (dealers will give you about 60 percent of guide prices). Many lesser-condition cards—especially new cards—can't be sold at all (even those dealers who do buy them for a pittance will act as if they're doing you a favor to take them off your hands).

So if you want to invest in cards, you should go with mint. But you can build a good collection with old nonmint cards if you're not concerned about reselling them. In fact, many people collect only the lower-priced VG-, good-, or poor-condition cards. If you crave a 1956 Willie Mays just to have and look at, why not pay $10 for a good-condition card instead of $100? It also makes sense to buy old tobacco cards in good condition for $3 or $4—among the best bargains in the hobby—instead of paying $30 for the same cards in mint condition. Nonmints are a good way to build a fine collection of old cards that have some value and some investment potential.

MEGACARDS

They catch your eye in the hobby-magazine ads. They sit majestically by themselves on shelves at card shops. They are the dealers' pride and joy at conventions. They are the megacards, single mint-condition cards with high price tags. They are the 1933 Goudey Ruths and Gehrigs, the 1911 Cobb and 1909 Mathewson tobacco cards, the 1940 Joe DiMaggio, the 1952 Mickey Mantle, the 1967 Tom Seaver. You see them inside the dealer's locked glass showcase, you sigh, and you walk away. Well, walk back.

The megacard can be a great investment. In 1987, the prices for almost every card then worth $300 jumped significantly. That may never happen again because 1987 was a watershed year in the hobby. But even if your megacard goes up in value an average of just 10 percent a year, which isn't unreasonable, your $1,000 card could be worth $1,100 in a year and $2,000 in ten years. (Always keep in mind that these are dealer prices, so if you buy a $1,000 card you will have to wait until its book value goes to about $1,400–1,500 before a dealer would buy it from you for more than $1,000.)

Which high-priced cards should you buy as investments? You should buy cards that not only have had a large price increase since 1985, when the card hobby really took off, but *also* continue to have strong yearly rate increases instead of leveling off. Choose cards that will go up significantly after you buy them because you have to compensate for the difference between what you paid a dealer and what the dealer will eventually pay to get it back.

Look at our set charts at the end of this book to see the Spring 1988 and projected Spring 1989 prices for the highest-priced cards for each set. Pay particular attention to which cards are expected to have solid price increases since last spring and which are stuck on their high prices. And be wary of—which doesn't mean you have to stay away from—Mickey Mantle cards, which are listed prominently on all lists. They have continued to go up in value, but since their prices are already so high and Mantle cards have flooded the market, their rate of increase has significantly decreased in the last year, and most experts predict that his cards may suddenly stall completely.

OLD CARDS

When asked which pre-1970 cards sell best, Alan "Mr. Mint" Rosen, the card hobby's most famous dealer, smiled. "All of them," he said, succinctly summing up what investors already know: *All old cards sell and sell well.*

Old cards are in demand for two reasons. First: today's adult monied collectors feel nostalgic about cards they had in their youth, or their fathers and grandfathers had in their collections. Equally important: they are rare. Today there are five major card companies. In the early thirties, there was just one, Goudey; there was just Play Ball in 1939 and 1940; Bowman was alone in 1949 and 1950; and Topps had the card field to itself from 1956 to 1981, with the exception of 1963 when Fleer put out a set. Today it's estimated that 5 billion cards are produced each year. In 1956, Topps, the only maker, produced about 300 million cards. That means there are seventeen times as many Boggses and Mattinglys produced today as Mantles and Kalines were produced in 1956. Furthermore, the great majority of old cards were tossed out when the kid went away for the weekend or grew up, by mothers cleaning out closets. Perhaps only 30 million from each set still exist today, or just five or six cards for every contemporary collector. And the number of those cards that are still in mint condition is significantly lower. The high prices and demand for mint pre-1970 cards reflects the recognition that the supply of old cards in mint condition will continue to dwindle. Pre-1960 cards are already getting more difficult to find. Prices will continue to increase as more and more of these cards are withdrawn from the market and hoarded. So look for good deals *now*. It's likely you can resell the old mint cards in 1990 at 20 percent profit—but they would be great to keep in a collection.

What old cards should you buy? We suggest high-priced cards (see our previous section on megacards), low-priced tobacco cards, New York ballplayers, regional favorites, Hall of Famers; and early cards (some megacards) of retired sure-shot and possible future Hall of Famers such as Jim Palmer, Pete Rose, Reggie Jackson, Gaylord Perry, Tom Seaver, Phil Niekro, Don Sutton, Steve Carlton, Joe Morgan, Rollie Fingers, Rod Carew, Tony Perez, Ferguson Jenkins, Jim Bunning, Phil Rizzuto, Nellie Fox, and Gil Hodges.

Since 50 percent of all card collectors and investors live in the New York area, New York–player cards (as well as memorabilia) sell well. Old Yankees, Dodgers, Giants, and Mets are hot now and will continue to be. Even nonsuperstars of New York teams command high prices; a consistent best-seller is Sal Maglie, even though he isn't in the Hall of Fame. "The Barber" had the distinction of pitching for the Giants, Dodgers, and Yankees, and that's enough to make him popular in the hobby.

Other areas of the country have their own stars. In Chicago, Ernie Banks is king; in Detroit it's Al Kaline; in St. Louis, Stan Musial reigns supreme. While Red Sox cards are not worth a whole lot in New York, they sell at higher than guide prices throughout New England. If you're a Sox fan, it might even pay to come to a New York card show or card shop to buy your Boston players.

NEW CARDS

New cards are much harder to judge than old cards. And the ultimate crapshoot is in rookie cards. Will Gregg Jefferies develop into a superstar to justify the $8 being charged for his Donruss and Fleer rookie cards? Will Eric Davis rebound from his substandard 1988 season to bring his Topps rookie card up from the $10 it dropped to after being priced at $17 in 1987? We mustn't forget those collectors who snapped up Minnesota Twins cards after the Twins won the 1987 World Series and were burned in 1988 when the Twins dropped in the standings and their cards went nowhere.

The best advice we can give you on new and recent cards is to buy IBM—proven players—and speculate carefully on new players. Stars who have performed consistently in the past will probably continue to do so. Their cards will go up a bit each year, particularly their rookie cards. But realize that after the initial jump of a rookie card, it will probably level off until the player concludes what may be a 15-year career. Players rarely keep their momentum over an entire career—even a Mattingly will falter some years (as he did in 1988), causing a decrease in movement of his cards at book prices, followed by a decrease in prices for those cards.

Buy new players with caution to guard against flash-in-the-pan seasons. Buy hitters not pitchers, because few pitchers have several good years in a row from the start or avoid career-threatening injuries; buy sluggers rather than singles hitters (except for Wade Boggs). And even then there are no sure things. It's even dangerous to buy 1,000-card lots of a player who hits 49 homers his first year and 32 his second year. We doubt it will happen because he seems to be a legitimate star, but what if Mark McGwire hits only 20 homers

in 1989? We expect him to become another Harmon Killebrew, but maybe he won't. It's important to think of a player's
long-term career if you're planning on making a long-term
investment. So few players actually reach superstardom (as
McGwire did as a rookie) and remain there.

Among current ballplayers, only a few have the talent and/
or stats to have a shot at the Hall of Fame. Those are the
players you should invest in: George Brett, Don Mattingly,
Dave Winfield, Jose Canseco, Wade Boggs, Mark McGwire,
Ellis Burks, Gary Carter, Jim Rice, Mike Greenwell, Kirby
Puckett, Dwight Gooden, Bruce Sutter, Roger Clemens, Jack
Morris, Robin Yount, Cal Ripken, Jr., Eddie Murray, Fer-
nando Valenzuela, Orel Hershiser, Rickey Henderson, Tim
Raines, Darryl Strawberry, Tony Gwynn, Mike Schmidt, Eric
Davis, Nolan Ryan, Ryne Sandberg, Dale Murphy, Goose Gos-
sage, Carlton Fisk, Andre Dawson, Wally Joyner, Dwight
Evans, George Bell, and the woefully underpriced Ozzie
Smith, who someday will be discovered by the card hobby
because he has been baseball's highest-salaried player, the
top vote-getter for All-Star games, and is definitely Hall of
Fame bound.

ERROR AND VARIATION CARDS

Every year, there is much excitement when collectors discover things amiss on certain cards. It could be that a player's
name isn't spelled correctly, or that the guy in the photo
doesn't match the name; a player's stats are incorrect; a photo
has been reversed and a righthanded pitcher is suddenly a
southpaw; or, as in the case of Billy Ripken's "X-rated" 1989
Fleer card, something is in the photo that the cameraman

missed. In many cases, the card company will stop printing these error cards and issue new, corrected cards—the error cards then become known as "variations." In other cases, the error is considered so insignificant that the card company will let it stand—the "error card" becomes a permanent part of the set.

When word gets out, there is usually a flurry of buying and selling and these cards shoot up quickly in price (unless it's an insignificant error on an insignificant player). But beware: There have been numerous error cards and very few have values significantly higher than if there were no error; ironically, corrected cards are valued higher than variations. So they are usually a lot of excitement about nothing.

Still, you shouldn't ignore them; if you find one in a pack, hold on to it. You may also consider buying or trading for them if you don't have to give up much. We say this because there's always the chance that one of these cards will maintain a high price and that, since they're a fun theme for a collection, you will always be able to find someone who will want to buy them from you at good prices.

ROOKIE CARDS

Somewhere in the misty dark ages of baseball card collecting—the early 1980s—the powerhouses of the industry (people who until a year before were doing something else for a living) decided that a player's most valuable card had to be his rookie card. The experts decided that a "first" card must be the most valuable because it was like a first-edition book. That idea has been refined over the years because players' first cards sometimes appear in a traded, or updated, set at the end of the season (such as Dwight Gooden in 1984) or appear in one company's annual set but not the others (Jose Canseco appeared only in Donruss and Fleer cards in 1986). Earlier, it was clearer. The player appeared in Topps, and that was his rookie card.

Rookie cards make up the centerpiece of the hobby. While many Mickey Mantle cards sell at over $100, it is only Mickey's rookie cards (Topps 1952, Bowman 1951) that command the staggering price tags. Tom Seaver's rookie 1967 card sells at $400, but his second-year card is just $90. Eric Davis's 1985 Donruss rookie card goes at $25, his 1986 card at $5. The rookie is the premier card. So beware of dealers who explain they're selling Roger Maris's sophomore card at the rookie-card price because "it is a much better-looking card."

Rookie cards have climbed higher and faster than any other type of cards. In 1985, Mantle's 1951 Bowman sold at $400. At this writing, it retails at $4,700. Hank Aaron's rookie went at $175 in 1985. It sells for about $500 today. Ernie Banks was $55 in 1985 and is $300 today. Pete Rose was at $300 in 1985, at $550 today. Mike Schmidt was at $65 in 1985, at $150 today.

Obviously, a good investment would be to snap up all the rookie cards of first-year players and sell them for a small fortune. After all, in 1985 you could have bought a Topps Mark McGwire Olympic card at 3¢. Today, each is worth $17. If you spent $100 on McGwires in 1985, you'd have $57,000 worth of cards today.

Ah, but whom should you buy? There are 70 or 80 rookie cards each year. If you spend $100 on each of them, you'll spend $7,000–8,000. So be selective. Pick the few best players and stock up on them (you can buy 100-card lots from dealers at very good prices). The card companies hire top sportswriters and consultants to help you do this. For instance, Donruss has New York *Daily News* veteran baseball writer Bill Madden select its annual Rated Rookies. Topps and Fleer and Score also have special rookie prospects. That's a good jumping-off point.

Better still, keep an eye out yourself for these newcomers. Then you'll be prepared when Ty Griffin, Sandy Alomar, Jr., Dave West, Ken Griffey, Jr., Robin Ventura, and Jim Abbott hit the majors. (One safe bet is to buy the Topps Olympic players set every four years.) You can follow minor league stars in *Baseball America,* which comes out twenty times a year, *The Sporting News, USA Today, Tuff Stuff,* and several daily papers and hobby magazines. If you notice that rookie Joe Bipp hit .400 for three consecutive years as he went from A to AAA ball, then you should get your money ready for when his rookie card is issued. However, if you see Joe is slumping at .220 and none of the card companies has designated him a top rookie prospect, then he's not such a sure bet.

If you've found Joe has been selected by Donruss and various sportswriters as a rated rookie and Joe hits .400 again in spring training, prompting the big league team to sell a star to make room for him, then buy Joe. You'll make a fortune if you buy a 100-card lot of his rookie card and he has an outstanding rookie season, capped by hitting six or seven homers in the World Series. But what happens to your investment if you hold off, hoping for another fantastic year before selling his cards, and Joe damages a leg in an accident and his average plummets to .220 in his second year and .190 in his third year when pitchers discover he can't hit sliders? Remember that Joe Charboneau went from Rookie of the Year to Double A the next season. This is a big, big problem with rookie cards. Players fall victim to the sophomore jinx or prove to be just an average major leaguer. Check baseball history: very few rookie stars, including Rookies of the Year, go on to Hall of Fame careers. Moreover, you can pick a winner and still lose: the card of Detroit catcher Matt Nokes shot up like a rocket in his rookie 1987 season, but it plunged in his sophomore season although he has confirmed he is a top-notch player.

The rookie market is hot and you will be tempted to jump in, even if only to round up the rookie stars on your favorite team. A general rule is to pick hitters instead of pitchers, because they have less chance of getting seriously hurt; however, if one-handed Angels pitching prospect Jim Abbott makes it big and he becomes a national sensation, his first card, his Olympic team card—No. 1 in Topps 1988 updated set—should become the hottest card in the market. Another rule is to pick home run hitters such as Mark McGwire and Jose Canseco—although nonslugger Wade Boggs is very popular with collectors, and we doubt homers alone will ever make the rookie card of underpublicized Blue Jay slugger Fred McGriff a hot commodity. Finally, pick stars from New York and California, the coast-to-coast investment, because both are glamor areas with big baseball followings. This is to protect your rookie investment. Even if your player dips a bit in his sophomore year, the many fans of his team will still want his card. A warning: when a rookie card peaks after a player has been in the majors for two, three, or four years, it will not go up much more until that player nears retirement or we enter a new decade and all old cards go up. Players just cannot keep up the momentum of a great rookie year, and their rookie card prices will at some point stall as a result.

TOP-PRICED ROOKIE & FIRST-YEAR CARDS

*(**Bow**-Bowman, **D**-Donruss, **F**-Fleer, **FU**-Fleer Update, **T**-Topps, **TM**-Topps Minis, **Topps Tr**-Topps Traded)*

SPRING 1988 PRICE

Mantle T1952
$6,500

Mantle Bow1951
$4,700

Mays Bow1951
$1,100

Mays T1952
$800

Rose T1963
$550

Aaron T1954
$500

Seaver T1967
$400

Clemente T1955
$325

Banks T1954
$300

Kaline T1954
$300

Koufax T1955
$250

Maris T1958
$225

BRobinson T1957
$200

RJackson T1969
$200

Schmidt T1973
$150

Yastrzemski T1960
$150

Carew T1967
$125

Ryan T1968
$125

Gibson T1959
$125

Bench T1968
$125

Stargell T1963
$100

Killebrew T1955
$100

FRobinson T1957
$100

Carlton T1965
$100

Uecker T1962
$90

Clemens FU1984
$75

Drysdale T1957
$65

McCovey T1960
$65

Wills T1967
$65

GBrett TM1975
$65

Murphy T1977
$65

Mattingly Don1984
$65

Gooden FU1984
$65

Marichal T1961
$60

Brock T1962
$60

Carter TM1975
$60

Rice TM1975
$60

Puckett FU1984
$60

PNiekro T1964
$55

SPRING 1988 PRICE (continued)

Garvey T1971
$55

GBrett T1975
$50

Palmer T1966
$45

Yount TM1975
$45

Sutton T1966
$40

Carter T1975
$40

Rice T1975
$40

Aparicio T1956
$35

Hunter T1965
$35

TPerez T1965
$35

KHernandez TM1975
$35

EMurray T1978
$35

BWilliams T1961
$30

JMorgan T1965
$30

Munson T1970
$30

Boggs T1983
$30

Mattingly F1984
$30

Yount T1975
$30

Parrish &
Murphy T1978
$30

RHenderson T1980
$28

Molitor &
Trammell T1978
$28

Mattingly T1984
$27

Winfield T1974
$25

EDavis Don1985
$25

KHernandez T1975
$25

Dawson T1977
$25

Strawberry Topps
Tr1983
$24

Saberhagen FU1984
$20

Boggs Don1983
$17

Boggs F1983
$17

EDavis F1985
$17

McGwire T1985
$17

Gwynn T1983
$16

DwEvans T1973
$15

Parker T1974
$15

Strawberry Don1984
$15

Guidry T1976
$12

Darling FU1984
$12

Clemens Don1985
$12

CRipken T1982
$12

EDavis T1985
$10

Oliva T1963
$10

JClark T1977
$10

Saberhagen Topps
Tr1984
$10

Gooden D1985 $10	Raines T1981 $8.50	OSmith T1979 $7
Strawberry F1984 $10	Clemens F1985 $8	GeBell T1982 $7
Clemens T1985 $10	Puckett Don1985 $8	Canseco Don1986 $7
Strawberry T1984 $9		

MINOR LEAGUE CARDS

Perhaps the most explosive market in the hobby is the minor league card. These cards and sets don't attract much notice in the 23 major league cities and the suburban towns around them; why bother with the New York-Penn League when you can see the Yankees? Why bother with the Las Vegas Stars when you can see the San Francisco Giants? But too many collectors and investors forget that the minor leagues dominate much of the sporting press outside the major league markets—totally dominate it. The Utica Blue Sox, in Utica, New York, on a postgame day, get five or six times the space the New York Mets and New York Yankees get *combined* in most upstate New York newspapers. Baseball in upstate New York *is* the minor leagues. The same is true for the Carolinas, Florida, the Deep South, the Southwest, and parts of the Midwest. And major league fans should envy minor league fans—out there in baseball's America, you can usually sit right behind home plate or the dugouts, get free autographs from players before the game and chat with the manager if you like—all for about $3–4 a ticket.

Minor league sets have been around for years, but it wasn't until about 1985 that they began to proliferate, with the two top suppliers being Pro Cards and TCMA. There are smaller publishers, such as the Star Co., of Cherry Hill, New Jersey, that also do nice work.

While minor league team sets and cards do not have the details and records that major league cards have, they are usually quite impressive, with lush color photographs of the players, and sell for about $3 per team set. They are valuable because almost all major league stars play at least one year in the minors. A superstar's card from a minor league set predates his official major league "rookie" card and is worth a lot. Don Mattingly's Columbus Clipper card sells at over $20, close to his $27 "rookie" card. Benito Santiago played for the Las Vegas Stars; that team's set, because he's in it, shot from $3 to $9 in one year. Gregg Jefferies's minor league card sells for as much as his major league "rookie" card. Until late in his MVP 1988 campaign, Jose Canseco's minor league card (many have been autographed by Canseco) sometimes sold at $10 unsigned and $18 signed. His Donruss 1986 "rookie" card went for about $7 in early 1988 and then went up over ten times when he became the first player to hit 40 homers and steal 40 bases in a season.

The trouble with investing in minor league sets, though, is that, like rookie cards, you have to pick a player you think is going to the majors. It's not smart to pay $3 for each of 50 minor league team sets if none of those sets' players make it big in the majors. How do you track minor leaguers? The same way you track rookies. Read *The Sporting News, Tuff Stuff,* local newspapers, and *USA Today.* As we said before, the most valuable publication you can get is *Baseball America,* the Durham, North Carolina, newspaper devoted to minor league baseball. There's also the minor-league-card newsletter: *Mary Huston's Monthly Minor League Price Guide,* out of North Lima, Ohio.

Because of limited print runs and passionate collectors,

minor league sets and individual cards are good investments. This is especially so if those teams and players are affiliated with the New York and L.A. teams or teams such as the A's and Red Sox who have recently turned out stars in their minor league system; or if the players (such as Gregg Jefferies, Al Leiter, Jose Canseco, Ken Griffey, Jr., and Sandy Alomar, Jr.) are getting an inordinate amount of publicity at the minor league level.

Minor league sets can be bought at most card shows, and for local teams, card shops. Dealers will likely have minor league cards for current major league stars, even if they don't have the other players on those farm teams. For a larger selection (and there are hundreds of sets on the market now) you should check the hobby publications for mail-order ads. *Tuff Stuff* often gives out a free minor league card set of a team with a top prospect when you order a subscription. The best place to buy card sets is at minor league parks. Then you may be able to get autographs on the cards a few minutes after your purchase. It hasn't really been determined if autographs devalue minor league cards, as they do major league cards, but in any case, it will be nice to have an *early* autograph of a star player in your collection.

Incidentally, the success of minor league sets has encouraged several colleges and major conferences to issue sets of their baseball teams. Buy the sets of college powerhouses—Stanford, Oklahoma, Oklahoma State, Texas, Arizona State, USC, Miami, etc.—and you are bound to wind up with future major league stars.

BLACK VS. WHITE PLAYER CARDS

It is a fact of the hobby that 99.5 percent of all collectors are white. Despite the high number of current black superstars such as Darryl Strawberry, Dwight Gooden, Dave Winfield, Eric Davis, Rickey Henderson, George Bell, Ellis Burks, Ozzie Smith, Tony Fernandez, and others, few black Americans, adults or boys, collect cards of black stars. And unfortunately, racism exists in the card collecting hobby as it does everywhere else.

Because most collectors are white, and because of racial biases that dealers pander to by promoting only white player cards, the cards of black superstars are always worth less than the cards of equally skilled white stars. The most glaring examples are the 1951 Bowman Mantle and Mays rookie cards and the 1952 Topps Mantle and Mays rookie cards. In each year, Mantle cards are worth several times what the Mays cards are worth, even though Willie hit more home runs than Mickey (660 to 536), had a higher lifetime batting average (.302 to .298), and had at least an equal career and as passionate a following. In other years, with other black and white stars, the story is the same. White stars are always valued more highly than blacks. Why does there continue to be more movement on Roger Clemens cards than Dave Stewart cards? How could George Bell's 1982 rookie card be worth only $7 after he won the 1987 MVP title when the rookie card of MVP runner-up Alan Trammell is worth $28?

"People just don't want to invest in black stars," says one major national dealer. "I tell everybody who asks my advice on investing to buy New York and buy white."

Why?

Again, the hobby is 99.5 percent white. Also, most card

shows are in suburban towns, where most of the residents are white. Most Little Leagues, the centerpiece of youth baseball in America, are in suburban towns, which are mostly white.

There is economics. "Look at statistics," says Ron Durham, one of the few blacks who owns a card shop (in Dumont, N.J.) and the successful promoter of the 1988 National Convention. "Blacks just do not have the spendable income whites do. Whatever extra money there is in the black family goes to pay bills, not buy baseball cards."

Many black stars are angry about the lack of black card collectors, but it goes deeper than that. "I'm saddened that there's a declining number of American blacks playing the game itself," says Don Newcombe, ex-Brooklyn Dodger pitching great. "We have blacks from Cuba and the Dominican Republic, but not from the U.S. We see all our eleven- and twelve-year-old black Little Leaguers turning to football and basketball, not baseball. They don't play baseball, so they don't collect cards. I'm afraid that in ten years there will be no black Americans playing major league baseball at all."

The solutions are varied, from more black stars supporting card shops owned by blacks to more black managers to more black companies sponsoring baseball events.

"Obviously, there's a problem in the lack of black collectors and the undervalued black cards," says former Cleveland Indians slugger Larry Doby. "What we have to do is get black stars to support the card industry, and I don't mean just showing up to sign autographs—I mean big involvement with black entrepreneurs. We need seed money to get blacks interested in what obviously is a profitable industry. We've got to make more blacks aware of the dollar potential here."

Lou Brock, the all-time base-stealing champ, thinks American baseball needs a whole new look: "We need more black managers and coaches, black owners, black batboys, vendors, ticket-takers, clubhouse personnel, and front office executives. We need more black sportswriters and broadcasters. We've got to let kids know, by letting them just look at the game with their own eyes and see these people we need, that baseball is an American game, a black and white game, not just a white game."

But should you invest in black player cards, given all this negativism? If you are smart, you will.

There will be enlightenment in the baseball card and collectibles hobby in the next few years, perhaps aided by the presence of Bill White as the new President of the National League. All it will take is for dealers to start promoting black player cards as they do the cards of charismatic white players. They are incredibly foolish not to have done so already; consider that while mostly white people go to major league games, the top vote-getters on fan-selected All-Star Game rosters have been black players such as Rod Carew, Reggie Jackson, Darryl Strawberry, and Ozzie Smith. But stubborn dealers will come around when they need to inject new excitement into the hobby. Just as major league baseball was integrated for economic (as well as moral) reasons—white owners realized they needed black players to increase attendance—the hobby will eventually need movement on black player cards to avoid losing momentum. Dealers will push black player cards—they will act as if they just *discovered* them—when interest flags (and it will, because the current fads are just that, fads) in the rookie, minor league, and white superstar cards they are now heavily promoting. So be prepared for the boom. Even if there isn't one in the next few years, it will be good to have cards of Jackie Robinson, Satchel

Paige, Willie Mays, Bob Gibson, and today's black superstars in your collection.

CARDS INVESTORS SHOULD STAY AWAY FROM

The worst investment in cards is the box set. You've seen them everywhere from K mart to Woolworth's to Newberry's. You get 33 star cards in some sort of theme box, such as "Rookies" or "Pitchers and Hitters." They sell at $2–4. They are nice to have (the Circle K home-run hitters set is a gem) but you should realize that they are useless as an investment. Yes, we know the trade publications tell you that last year's box set has gone up from $2 to $4. They make that figure up to keep you buying box sets; although these publications are reliable, remember that much of their revenue comes from dealers and card stores who want to sell you box sets. Case closed.

The second-worst investment is Drake's Cakes cards. Everybody falls into the Drake's trap. You run out and buy nine or ten boxes of Drake's cakes, doughnuts, coffee cakes, or whatever and carefully cut out the panels with two to four cards on them. The whole set, the trade magazines tell you, can be worth $25 a year later. Just try and sell one to somebody. There's just no market for these. Don't be fooled.

Another bad investment, as we have mentioned, are common cards of any kind. You see ads all the time for these, once again backed up by the trade publications. Are all 1952 Topps commons worth $20 or more? Are all 1951 Bowmans worth $8 or more? Are old cards worth money just because they're old, even if they're commons? No. They are great cards to have, but no one will buy these cards from you unless they're trying to fill out a set.

Another waste of investment money is in reprints. You've seen ads for "Authentic Reprints," a term that makes no sense. For just $10 you can get reprints of a set whose originals would cost $5,000. So why do the reprints cost only $10? Because they're useless. If you like the way the cards look, whether it's '52 Topps reprints or T-3s or Bowmans, go ahead and pay your $20 or $4 or whatever they want. Just don't expect to sell them to anyone.

What about the 3-D Sportflics? Walk down the other side of the street on this one. Nobody, but nobody, collects Sportflics. Why they keep producing them each year is a mystery akin to who built the Mayan pyramids. Sportflics don't sell, and if they do sell, they don't resell. Nobody even saves these 3-D wonders. Don't expect them to stay on the market, either. The same company started the impressive Score last year, we believe, as the card set to push when Sportflics goes to the card shop in the sky.

BUYING
BASEBALL
COLLECTIBLES

We saw an elderly man show a collector a ball that had been in his closet since the 1930s. He asked hopefully if it was worth anything. The collector studied the ball, which had, in crisp and clear writing, the signatures of Babe Ruth, Lou Gehrig, Tony Lazzeri, Connie Mack, Heinie Manush, Lefty Grove, Lefty Gomez, Jimmie Foxx, and four or five others. Yes, it was worth something. Maybe $3,000, probably more. The man gasped. The rest of us wondered what else was in his closet.

Thousands of people have wonderful pieces of sports memorabilia—new and old—tucked away in their closets, attics, basements, and garages. Balls, bats, autograph books, score-cards, gloves, pins, one-of-a-kind items, etc. If they played baseball as kids, the chances are good they have pieces of equipment lying around—their mothers may have kept them as keepsakes. If they went to a ballgame, twenty years ago or just last season, they may have ticket stubs. They may have stashed away the *Boy's Life* magazines they bought in the twenties, featuring many beautifully illustrated baseball stories and ads with players such as Babe Ruth and Dazzy Vance. Or they may have accidentally walked off with the airplane's copy of *Sports Illustrated* with Pete Rose, Reggie Jackson, or Don Mattingly on the cover. Anyone who ever got an autograph, or who got hold of or took a picture of an athlete, or who clipped a newspaper article about a sports event has a genuine piece of sports memorabilia. And it's all worth something.

While everyone knows that baseball cards have become extremely valuable and a better investment than most stocks, relatively few people are aware that baseball collectibles are climbing in value, too—often at a quicker rate than cards. What is particularly exciting is that the majority of collec-tibles, unlike cards, have not been retrieved but still wait to be discovered. Great memorabilia comes out of the closet and into public view a little at a time, and it's a thrill for all collectors when a valuable or nostalgia-causing item that no one knew existed is placed on the market.

Memorabilia is leaping in value because it is connected to real events. Autographs, scorecards, and player-used bats and gloves are part of baseball history and the America of the second half of the nineteenth century and almost 90 years of the twentieth. To hold a Ty Cobb game-used bat, with Ty's nicely scrawled autograph at the end of it, is to hold the game of baseball itself. The old balls, yellowed from the march of time, are lovely pieces of Americana, and the signatures on them leap out at you like faded memories of youth. The illustrations in *Harper's* and the *London News,* depicting games and players from 1885 to the turn of the century, make that era come alive.

Amazingly, these remnants of our national pastime are available. You can buy Napoleon Lajoie's bat or Roger Hornsby's glove, or the cleats of stolen-base king Lou Brock. If you have over $2,000 to invest in a product that will definitely go up in value, you can buy a 1935 poster advertising an upcoming Negro League game in which Satchel Paige will pitch, or a billboard poster of Babe Ruth selling equipment. You can get balls autographed by Ruth, and there are many out there, for $800 on up, or a Lou Gehrig game bat for $2,000 on up. A glove used by the Chicago Black Sox's greatest player, Shoeless Joe Jackson, recently sold for $5,000. Or you can spend the $5,000 on a uniform of a retired Hall of Famer such as Duke Snider. For that money, you could also buy up to 25 uniforms of current nonstar players.

More and more people are filling showcases with baseball memorabilia. Others are turning extra rooms or sections of basements, garages, and offices into mini-baseball-museums. If you are interested in building your memorabilia collection or starting from scratch, you should begin, of course, by retrieving all the memorabilia you already have. Don't forget that some nonsports publications such as *Life* and *Time* occasionally have a ballplayer on the cover—those pictures are enough to make them sports collectibles. Once you have taken stock of your own memorabilia, look through hobby magazines and plan visits to antique stores, collectibles stores, thrift shops (where you should find sports magazines), flea markets, garage sales, card shows, and some card shops.

We don't want to give the impression that collecting memorabilia should be the private domain of rich adult hobbyists and investors who are obsessed with possessing old, currently valuable items. Even if you are a kid, an adult with no inclination to spend a lot of money, or aren't interested in collecting anything older than you are, you can still become a certified memorabilia collector and have fun putting together a valuable collection.

Look around the next time you visit a card shop, card show, or museum. The $100 and $1,000 items you see are a previous generation's collection. Kids who got Babe Ruth autographs outside stadiums and Satchel Paige posters at Negro League games have, 50 years later, valuable items that make for an enviable collection. And too many card and memorabilia collectors today think they have to get similar 50-year-old items to have any collection at all. Nothing could be further from the truth.

Today's collectors can put together a collection that people 50 years from now will envy. In fact, we can guarantee you that people 10 or 20 years from now will offer to buy your collection at prices far greater than your initial investment. So in addition to buying 3¢ baseball cards and $18–20 card sets, purchase $2–4 posters, $4–15 autographs, and affordable equipment (which you can try to get autographed to increase its value), and go to promotion days, etc. If you choose the right items and right players, you can really put together a valuable collection. In 40 years, the Don Mattingly autograph you have in your hand may be as valuable as a Lou Gehrig autograph is today. You don't need a lot of money to put together a fine collection and good investment. But you do need a game plan.

Almost every type of baseball memorabilia is becoming increasingly popular and valuable. However, different memorabilia have different aesthetic and long-term investment values. Some are easy to acquire inexpensively, while other items are difficult to find and may be overpriced. Significantly, much memorabilia can be upgraded in value if *you* use your smarts. So read our lowdown on some of the most popular items to help you decide what to get, and how to get it conveniently and economically.

AUTOGRAPHS

Everyone has seen photos of Babe Ruth handing out autographs to the kids who followed him everywhere he went. We have all heard stories of Lou Gehrig's standing outside Yankee Stadium giving autographs to his young fans long after his teammates had rushed home. And if you went to games anytime before the eighties, you probably figured you had about a fifty-fifty chance of getting player autographs when they drifted over to the stands during warmups or when they walked through the stadium parking lot, before and after the game. But we all know times have changed. True, there are good-guy fan favorites such as Dale Murphy and Chris Sabo, eager-to-please rookies and bench warmers, and minor leaguers and college stars who are willing to sign anything thrust in front of them. But most major leaguers sign as few autographs as they can at the park without damaging their reputations, and others completely avoid fans and their Sharpies—except at card shows, when they get an appearance fee.

There are ways to get autographs without resorting to following a player into a restaurant bathroom, staking out his hotel lobby, handing him a ball and a pen while he is carrying his baby, or standing in front of his car with a baseball bat. As we said earlier, the easiest way to get player autographs (and autographed items) is through the mail. Many players won't respond or will take many months, others may ask for a small fee or a donation to a charity (a commendable tack), and some are flattered by autograph requests and immediately comply. Send a nice letter explaining you want the player's autograph for *your* permanent collection, send a self-addressed, stamped envelope, and send thank-you notes afterward.

Some ball clubs give out autographed photos of current players on request; others just send unsigned photos. Make autograph requests at the beginning of the season. If the teams don't have what you want, you can order autographs (and autographed items) from dealers and card show promoters who place ads in hobby publications. (Hobby-magazine readers will also offer autographs for sale, but since you have no way of knowing if those autographs are legitimate, beware.) Most likely the promoters, who have players signing autographs at their shows, will have lower prices than the dealers. But while each promoter will only be able to offer autographs of the few players at his particular show, the dealer will have a large selection, perhaps acquired when he promoted several past shows. Be patient. If you want an autograph of a living star player, you will be able to order it eventually through a promoter or get it yourself at a show. Baseball players are not like reclusive movie stars. There is no Greta Garbo figure who stays out of the public eye. Even gods such as Joe DiMaggio, Willie Mays, Hank Aaron, Mickey Mantle, and Ted Williams accept fees from promoters to sign autographs. (However, some big-name players like Don Mattingly don't like card shows and have drastically curtailed autograph sessions.)

Of course, it is much more satisfying to get autographs

from the players directly. And not just because you will know for sure that the autographs are authentic in a hobby where there is forgery. It's fun to meet ballplayers, if only for a few seconds. So why not make the attempt to get their autographs inside or outside the ballpark, even though you're likely to come up empty-handed? Even the biggest stars will occasionally sign autographs on the field. Edge over toward the dugout and be the first to ask. If you don't have your autograph book with you, toss him a ball, glove, cap, or scorecard—for some reason players like to catch things. You will have better luck at minor league parks, getting autographs of those players you expect will have standout major league careers.

If a player is making a special appearance at a school, supermarket, or bookstore, you can also make a special stop. If you are serious about collecting autographs, you might even consider spending a few days watching your favorite team in spring training, which means traveling to Arizona or Florida—as many baseball fanatics do. You will have much better access to players during spring camp when the pace is leisurely. Prospects tend to sign autographs because it makes them feel like big leaguers (and they're young enough to remember when they sought autographs from their baseball heroes), and veterans tend to be so bored with spring training that they sign autographs just to break the routine. The best place to get autographs of living Hall of Fame members is Cooperstown, New York, during the weekend of the annual induction ceremonies. There are two autograph sessions, one for those over 15, the other for those 15 and younger. You can get autographs of the all-time greats who appear for the ceremonies and visit the Hall of Fame and learn about them and the others. Definitely consider it for a weekend vacation, but make reservations at least six months in advance at local inns or the grand old Otesaga Hotel (the players all stay there).

If you must pay for an autograph of a star, the easiest way to acquire one personally is to stand in line at a card show. It's costly: you'll pay between $2 and $4 just to get into the show, then another $5 to $15 for an autograph. The show promoters charge this to recover the $5,000 to $15,000 they must pay each player to appear.

It's sad that baseball has become an industry in which the stars who used to sign for free now get a fee and fans must buy tickets for an autograph. But promoters argue, with some merit, that if they did not provide stars at shows most fans would never see them. What are the chances of bumping into DiMaggio at a restaurant, Mantle at an airport? Of course, if you do, the stars will give you an autograph for nothing. They charge for card shows like they charge for dinners or speeches. Besides, if you went to a game just to get an autograph, you'd pay $10 for the ticket, $4 to park, $5 for tolls and gas; a card show can actually be cheaper.

One suggestion, though—why can't promoters hold the line against big star fees? Jose Canseco can get by on $8,000 an afternoon instead of $15,000, can't he?

Despite the awkward autograph situation that exists, some of the stars are great at the autograph table. But some are miserable. There is no point standing in line for an hour, after having paid up to $15, to get the autograph of someone who makes it quite clear that he's only there because he's getting paid. So here's a rating list of a few players on the autograph circuit whom we've observed in action:

DUKE SNIDER—*A. A true gentleman. A kind and generous man who actually has a clause in his contract that forbids show promoters from rushing him when he chats with fans in line. Nice to everyone, and is flattered by those who have fond memories of the old Dodgers.*

JOE DIMAGGIO—*A. Has an aura all to himself. He shakes everyone's hand and smiles at you as if you've been life-long friends. He's particularly nice with kids—he has been known to give autographs to any youngster who wants one, not just those who bought tickets.*

WILLIE MAYS—*C. Not as bad as his reputation, but he's a surprisingly unelectrifying presence at card shows, where he's all business. Outside of that commercial setting, how-ever, he's very different—a real delight.*

WHITEY FORD—*A. A jovial and friendly man who laughs with adults as easily as with children.*

REGGIE JACKSON—*D. An abrasive, crude, arrogant man who throws autographed items back at fans, often won't even look at you, and tends to be late anyway. Meeting Reggie is an awful experience.*

ERNIE BANKS—*A. Mr. Cub is Mr. Autograph. A great friendly bear of a man who'll personalize anything you want.*

PETE ROSE—*D. Unpleasant and always in a big hurry. Barely smiles. A surprise dud.*

DARRYL STRAWBERRY—*A. Surprisingly glib and talkative. He wants to have a good image with kids.*

LENNY DYKSTRA—*B+. Good with kids. Lots of smiles. A funny character. Try to get him to talk because he has a weird vocabulary.*

JOHNNY MIZE—*B+*. *The Big Cat is a bit gruff at first, but once you've broken the ice, he's fine.*

LOU BROCK—*A−*. *A real gentleman.*

MAURY WILLS—*A*. *He's so eager to please fans he'll even help your child with his batting stance.*

BILL SKOWRON—*B+*. *Moose looks tough, but is a pussycat.*

DON NEWCOMBE—*B+*. *A personable guy and superbright.*

MONTE IRVIN—*B*. *Must talk to him first to get him going.*

RICKEY HENDERSON—*A*. *Just terrific. Fans won't boo him here.*

MICKEY MANTLE—*A*. *The Mick gets better and better at interacting with people and he's good, but his lines are too long to permit much time. Promoters rarely let him sign bats because that slows down the lines.*

WARREN SPAHN—*A*. *Another beautiful guy who'll personalize anything, even undersides of caps.*

RAY DANDRIDGE—*C+*. *A little gruff and quiet, but hey, you'll be too at age 83.*

BILLY WILLIAMS—*B*. *New to signing, but shows promise.*

RALPH BRANCA—*B*. *Still grimaces when Bobby Thomson is mentioned . . . of course everyone mentions Thomson.*

CATFISH HUNTER—*B*. *Friendly, but lukewarm. Has aura.*

TOMMY HENRICH—*A*. *One-time Yankee outfielder is a sure thing with fans at shows. He's still "Old Reliable."*

MICKEY OWEN—*A*. *A nice guy who doesn't even get mad if you mention he dropped Henrich's third strike in the*

World Series. Talks a lot about the past. Has many anec-
dotes.

BOB LEMON—*C—. Dull. Doesn't go out of his way to be*
friendly.

EARLY WYNN—*C. He claimed he'd even throw at his*
mother if she hit against him. Even some of that meanness
might enliven his appearances at shows. Quiet.

LUKE APPLING—*A—. Is 83, going on 13. A lively, chatty*
guest. Make a short stop at his table. Full of anecdotes,
jokes.

STEVE CARLTON—*B+. He'll say more to you than he's said*
to the press in 20 years—surprisingly talkative and nice.

BILLY HERMAN—*A—. A lovely guy who's happy to talk*
about the old Dodgers. This is why we loved the Dodgers.
Very knowledgeable and analytical about old and current
players.

The autograph craze really took off only in 1987, so there
is no telling how much autograph prices will increase—just
that they will increase. Autographs are a sound long-term
investment, but remember that even if a star player's autograph doubles in value in five years, it will probably be much
less valuable than his most expensive baseball card if that
should also double in value during that time. This is surely
true of former players. One exception is the first- or second-
year player who has had excellent but not phenomenal seasons and has potential for a great career, a player such as
Ellis Burks. While his card will sell for $1.75–3, his auto-

graph will go for a slightly higher price, in the $4–8 range. Nevertheless, if he becomes a superstar in his third year, his rookie card may go up into double figures, but his autograph will go up only a dollar or two, if at all. Only in the distant future will the autograph prices reflect a great career—perhaps only when the player has both retired and stopped signing autographs. Another consideration: there are no single-signature (as opposed to multiplayer and team-signature) autographs for sale that even compare in value to the highest-priced cards. For instance, Babe Ruth's most expensive cards from the early-thirties Goudey sets are valued at four times more than his rare autographs. But autographs do have increasing value, so if you accumulate *many* of them (particularly of Hall of Famers), you will have an autograph collection in a few years that will compare in value to your card collection.

Right now, it's impossible to tell how much the prices of autographs of today's stars will increase in five, ten, or twenty years. The comparatively high prices of autographs of dead and elderly former stars is some indication, but remember that today's savvy collectors are more likely to hold on to autographs than baseball fans of the past. This means that current players' autographs will never become as rare. These collectors keep autographs because of their value, not only out of sentiment. So if you want to buy a current player's autograph, hold on to it for 20 years, and then sell it for a lot of money, realize that the only people who will need it 20 years from now are those who are too young to be fans today or haven't been born yet. That's still a big market, but not as big as the current market for the limited number of remaining autographs of past stars. Still, be assured that, even though hundreds of thousands of collectors are scooping them up, autograph values will increase from today's relatively inexpensive rates. The serious investor knows that autographs of dead or aging stars are the best investment because the number of their autographs is finite.

Autographs on pieces of paper, the backs of postcards, and index cards abound. (Long ago, players found it much easier to sign index cards at home and pass them out anytime a fan approached them. Stan Musial still does this.) Since they aren't extravagant items, they are much cheaper to buy than autographed balls and autographed photos. However, they can add a great deal to a collection. If you take an unsigned photo of a star, which you should be able to buy for $1.50– 2, and place it in a nice but inexpensive frame along with the simple autograph of that star, then the value of this collectible is much more than that of the three individual pieces combined. You can also place your autograph under a displayed model bat of that player to create a new, impressive collectible.

Autographed photos are usually of a single player. Double- and triple-player-autographed photos are obviously worth more, but usually only double or triple the single-player rate. The photo will be more valuable if a particular star is in it. As with all autographs and autographed items, signed photos of dead, elderly, or Hall of Fame–bound players are the best investments. Photos signed by famous players who have recently died or who have just been inducted into the Hall of Fame invariably shoot up in price. One heralded triple photo is the 1962 Mantle-Mays-Maris signed picture, which routinely sells at $200 and up. The high price is not due to Hall of Famers Mantle or Mays, but to Maris, because of his untimely death. When all three players are dead fifty years from now (yes, we're being very generous), the price of this photo could be astronomical.

Photos are perhaps the cheapest collectible on the market.

You can buy unsigned photos through the mail for about $2 each (don't pay more!), and even less if you buy in quantity. Mail order houses offer good prices and prompt service. Of course, the most fun comes from getting a star to sign your picture of him. If you attend a card show, you'll spend only $2 for the biggest star's photo (and save postage) and only $4 to $15 (the price charged for DiMaggio, Williams, Reggie Jackson, and a few others) for the signature of a player at the show.

Don't pay high prices for signed photos of living players. Don't be fooled by dealers who place their signed photos in fancy-looking but cheap frames. Go to a card show at which the star you want is present and have him sign your inexpensive photo. Or send your photo to the promoter and he'll get you the player's signature. Then buy yourself one of those cheap frames. Then you will have spent maybe $20 (including your entrance fee and autograph ticket) for what some dealers at the show are selling for $50–75, or more.

Autographed baseballs come in three categories: single signature, theme signature, and team ball. Single-signature balls, of course, contain only one signature. Theme-signature balls feature two or more players who are on one ball club or All-Star team, or who have accomplished similar feats. One currently popular theme ball has the signatures of homer-hitting A's Jose Canseco and Mark McGwire, who were back-to-back Rookies of the Year in 1986 and 1987. Another popular theme ball contains the signatures of former Dodger pitcher Ralph Branca and the Giant who homered to beat him for the 1951 pennant, Bobby Thomson. The team ball is the hardest for an individual to get personally because it contains almost all of the players on individual teams. But you can acquire these from dealers who order them in quantity from the teams.

Values of signed balls depend on who signed them. In the case of a theme ball, value depends on who signed them and the significance of their mutual feat or event. The values of team balls depend on the era and the significance of the teams. Here are a few prices of team balls:

1988   Blue Jays $50
1987   Twins (World Champs) $150
1985   Royals (World Champs) $150
1984   U.S. Olympic Team (with McGwire, Snider, and others) $350
1967   Angels $125
1966   Pirates (with Clemente and Stargell) $275
1951   Dodgers (with Robinson, Campanella, and Snider) $500
1942   Giants (with Ott and Hubbell) $225
1927   Yankees (World Champs, including Ruth and Gehrig) $2,000
1917   Giants (NL Champs) $1,500

Autographed balls are among the best collectibles. They can be the highlight of a small collection or the centerpiece of a large one. But are they also good investments? Yes and no. If you buy a Wally Joyner ball for $11, you must wait five or six years before it goes much past $20. The 1917 Giants ball listed above isn't going to go much higher than the $1,500 you can get it for today. This shouldn't discourage the collector from buying a Joyner ball or several of them—if he is satisfied with a modest return—or a 1917 autographed team ball that will make his entire collection more impressive. But the investment-minded collector should instead buy autographed balls of players and teams that are a part of baseball history/mythology. The value of memorabilia relating to the Chicago White (Black) Sox of 1919 went up with the release of the movie *Eight Men Out*. The same thing could happen with other memorabilia—including autographed balls—if there are hit movies (or best-selling books) about such players as Thurman Munson, Roger Maris, Moe Berg (catcher and part-time U.S. spy), Roberto Clemente, Tony Conigliaro, and Christy Mathewson; and such teams as the 1914 Braves, the 1927 Yankees, the St. Louis Cardinals "Gas House Gang," the Dodgers of 1947 and 1955, the 1961 Yankees, the Mets of 1962 and 1969, the A's of 1972–74, and the Big Red Machine of the seventies.

Don't buy an autographed ball of a living player from a dealer, unless his price is very low. Instead, buy an official major league ball for $5 (unless you are among the lucky ones who have a souvenir ball from a game you attended). Take it to a show and get a superstar to sign it for his autograph fee. Even better, get players like Reggie Jackson, Mickey Mantle, and Joe DiMaggio to sign the same ball. You've immediately turned $45 into $100. The fabled Willie Mays–Mickey Mantle–Duke Snider ball—all three New York centerfielders of the fifties together—goes for around $120. You could conceivably put one together yourself for about $35.

You can also make money by smart speculating. In April 1986, the team ball for the New York Mets, who were expected to win the NL pennant, sold for around $45. They won the World Series and now those balls sell for $240. So early in the season, buy the team ball of the club you predict will become World Champions. Remember that if one of the glamor teams (the Dodgers, Mets, Yankees, and to a lesser degree, Red Sox and Cubs) wins, the price of the ball will go very high—but those balls will cost more at the beginning of the year. If you choose a long shot to win the Series, the price of the autographed ball will be low. If your team should win, the price will certainly go up considerably, especially if a player on that team had a great year and won the MVP, Cy Young, or Rookie of the Year awards. Also, look for balls with signatures of rookies you think will become stars.

EQUIPMENT

Bats are great collectibles. Game-used bats are the best; they not only have the most character and provide the most pleasure—what fun it is to swing a bat once used by a big leaguer!—but also have the best investment potential, especially if they are autographed. You can purchase cracked and uncracked Louisville Sluggers and Adirondacks with or without the signature of the player who used it over the burn-in inscription in the fat part of the bat. We suggest you buy an unsigned game-used bat if it once belonged to a living player who is a frequent guest at card shows; you'll save many dollars by taking the bat to a card show and getting him to sign it. The value will likely jump $40 or $50, and even more for a Hall of Famer (though their unsigned bats will have been an expensive purchase). If you get a current player's bat signed and he has several good years, its value will definitely go up. (Promoter ads will inform you if the players will not be signing bats at certain shows.)

Investors interested in high returns should definitely think about purchasing game-used bats. Autographed game-used bats are quite valuable, with a $2,000+ price tag placed on uncracked bats of such luminaries as Babe Ruth and Ty Cobb, and the cracked bats of many former stars going for several hundred dollars each. The signed cracked and uncracked game-used bats of current stars go for between $50 and $125, and the cracked game-used bats of nonstars go for as low as $7. *All these prices will go up.*

Non-game-used bats of a player are mint-condition bats that may have his name inscribed. Players order dozens of these from the Hillerich & Bradsby Co., which makes Louisville Sluggers, to sign for promoters of card shows. They are worth less than game-used bats but are still great collectibles and good investments. Also, don't ignore old bats you can buy for $8 in sporting good stores. You can get one signed by a player, even if it's not his model bat. In fact, you may try to get several autographs on such a bat and really increase its value to make it an impressive collectible.

You can obtain bats of retired players, some with signatures, from dealers, collectors, and mail order houses, the biggest being Kenrich Bats in Temple City, California.

Unofficial bats, which you can buy in stores, are worth exactly what the stores charge, though you can increase their value by getting players to sign them. Players such as Darryl Strawberry and Will Clark will sign bats, but a signed store-bought bat is worth only about $50, compared to the $125 charged for their signed game-used bats. If you have a choice, ask the player to sign a game-used bat. But by no means should you not ask him to sign a store-bought bat just because the value is less. It, too, is a strong long-term investment.

Perhaps the most prized and expensive collectible is the whole or partial **uniform.** Only the hard-core collector should attempt to put together a uniform collection because uniforms are expensive and take up a lot of space. A jersey of a star such as Duke Snider costs $5,000. The jerseys of Babe Ruth, Lou Gehrig, and Ty Cobb are even more expensive. Even current common player jerseys sell for a minimum of $200, and players of the caliber of Pete O'Brien or Mel Hall sell for around $400. Uniforms are in demand, but we don't see much investment value for most of them since their prices rarely change, unless you can buy a new player's jersey or uniform and keep it until he becomes a superstar.

Player **gloves** are rarely on the market. The glove is a very personal item—players regard it as almost an extension of themselves. They will go through 72 bats in a season and not miss any when they break—but offer a reward for a missing glove. Upon retirement, most players literally "hang up their gloves." So if you can get your hands on (or into) a glove that is being sold at a decent price, *buy it*. Gloves are already valuable: those of Dwight Gooden and Pete Rose sell for $1,000, Shoeless Joe Jackson's glove goes for $5,000, and Bill Dickey's catcher's mitt is priced at $3,000.

Easier to collect, and nice pieces for a collection, are model gloves. These are gloves with a star's imprinted signature— a Don Mattingly glove, etc. Old ones are particularly valuable, especially if they are signed (a real rarity). Five prices: 1905 catcher's mitt, $125; 1920 fielder's glove, $100; 1935 first baseman's mitt, $90; 1950 Duke Snider model, $75; 1954 Robin Roberts model, $75.

Look for old gloves at flea markets and garage sales. Mothers have a way of selling your favorite glove without a touch of sentiment. They may wrongly assume that it's your autograph on the glove. Many a '50s autographed glove or '20s model glove have been purchased for $5 or less. Antique and collectibles stores may also have old gloves—and you should definitely look—but you will have to work hard to get a bargain there.

A recent phenomenon, the **batting glove,** which players discard after a few weeks, has become a nice collectible. If you can get hold of them cheaper than the going rate—they usually go for $15–30, and $75 for one signed by a star— take the chance. It's quite possible they will be valuable in a decade or two when improved batting gloves make these outmoded and a souvenir of our particular baseball era. You may want to take a shot because they are unusual items, and for adult collectors, quite affordable.

Cleats are also hard to come by because they are personal items. Like batting gloves and uniforms, the best way to get them is by mail order through trade publications. We suggest you buy cleats of base stealers, such as Lou Brock, Maury Wills, or Davey Lopes (a moderate $50).

Everyone should own **caps** of his or her favorite team. Forget the sun visors sold at stadiums, caps with adjustable straps, and hats with a product name. Don't settle for anything other than authentic hats. But realize that for a cap to go up in value, it will have to be signed (by a player, not you), or the team will have to change its logo or move to a different city—it happens.

Like cleats, caps are personal items for a player and are difficult to find for sale. Of course, an autographed cap is the most coveted. Most run $50 or more. The cap of a star, like Jack Clark, will go for about $65. They are nice collectibles. They are also good investments because they are so rare, but don't expect to get a high return on a cap of a current player for many years.

PROGRAMS AND SCORECARDS, YEARBOOKS, TICKETS AND POSTERS

These are some of the fun items in the hobby. You can get the new ones at the ballpark and by mail order. For older items, use mail order, go to a card show, or try collectibles or antique stores.

Of course, grab all you can at the ballpark. Buy programs/

scorecards *every* time you go to a game—especially a World Series or All-Star game. Seek out from dealers the programs/ scorecards of popular teams, especially pennant and World Series champions and New York teams. World Series and All-Star items from pre-1900 are the most expensive to purchase but also the best investments. Try to find a few programs from the late fifties going for about $10 each and keep all those new ones you accumulate at games. Too many people still toss out scorecards and programs—that's why they become rare quickly. Take note that program/scorecard prices drop for each decade as we move closer to the present. Prices for World Series and All-Star programs from the 1920s are $200+, while prices for those in the 1930s are below $200. Also notice that, with a few exceptions, the programs and scorecards from the early part of each decade are more expensive than those at the end. Because all old memorabilia go up decade by decade as we move into a new decade, we suggest that you buy the affordable items from the latter part of the decades. They probably won't become as valuable as the earlier programs, but we think that in the 1990s their prices will jump the same amount as the higher-priced items.

Buy your favorite team's yearbook every year at the ballpark, and also, if your team issues one in midseason, the updated yearbook (with a different cover), which may become even more valuable because not as many copies are printed. If you are interested in yearbooks as an investment, you should buy several yearbooks of your favorite team, with the intention of keeping at least one, and yearbooks of as many other teams as you can through dealers. Yearbooks dating back to 1914 are available, and since you'll never see more than a $400 price tag, they're relatively affordable, especially to the adult collector. As with programs, we suggest you buy yearbooks of champion and glamor teams, as well as first-

and last-year franchises; also buy those end-of-the-decade cheaper yearbooks, which should jump in value in the 1990s. Buy new yearbooks for about $5 today; they'll be worth $10–15 in ten years, $20–35 in twenty years, and $50 in thirty years. Because the return isn't very much on one yearbook, investors should buy in quantity. There will always be collectors of yearbooks, especially old ones in good condition, but don't expect to make a lot of money by selling one or two (in comparison to what you can get for World Series programs, for instance). Watch for yearbooks in comic and out-of-print book and magazine stores—open them up and see if there are any autographs on photos. If there are, don't mention this to the proprietor.

Ticket stubs are great collectibles, especially if you keep them with the scorecard of the game you attended. They are also extremely easy to collect and easy to save. Obviously, you can save several a year if you go to several games or if you sneakily hold on to the tickets of everyone who went to games with you. The most expensive regular-season tickets, those issued pre-1900, go for $150; those from the 1920s go for between $20 and $60, and those from the 1970s are valued at just $5–15. But if you get hold of a ticket of a classic game, perhaps a tribute to a retired player, a no-hitter, or a player's four-homer game, you have a memento whose value will rise. Tickets to World Series and All-Star games are worth more than regular-season tickets, but none is worth more than $300, and even those from the thirties aren't valued too high: $100–150 for a mint-condition All-Star game stub from the thirties and early forties, and $50 for a World Series stub from the same period. Because individual ticket stubs don't sell for very much money—full, unused tickets go for more—you will need to sell in quantity to get a good return. Whatever you get is an improvement on a $0 investment—consider ticket stubs free collectibles you get for buying admission to games.

Most teams will have giveaway days or nights on which fans receive posters of the team or its stars. These are usually quite nice and will have some added value if you get players to sign them. If your team is stingy, you can usually buy the team and star posters at the souvenir stand or through mail order. World Series, All-Star games, and star advertisement posters have the best investment potential, but it will take more than twenty years for their value to go up significantly. Put posters on the wall rather than keeping them rolled up in the closet for several decades, because you won't get much money for them anyway. There are better investments.

FIGURINES AND BOBBING HEAD DOLLS

There are two kinds of figurines. The first is the statue, which is usually made of plastic. The most valuable are the eighteen Hartland player statues that were produced in 1958–63. (The nineteenth Little Leaguer statue is not considered part of the set.) In mint condition, they range in price from the rare $450 Dick Groat (ironically, the only nonsuperstar) to the $75 Warren Spahn and Eddie Mathews. Thirty years ago, they sold for just $15. They are wonderful to own, but to buy them today as an investment is a mistake because they're expensive and probably won't go up enough for you to realize a profit. You could spend much less on the "new" Hartlands, authorized replicas. They sell for about $24 but don't have much investment value, despite the manufacturer's emphasis on how much the originals have gone up since they came on the market.

The other figurines are the popular ceramic statues, distributed by Sports Impressions. They are quite handsome and well-crafted, but at $125—and about $50 more for Mantle and $100 more for Mattingly—they are way overpriced. By comparison, you can buy a ceramic plate made in 1956 to commemorate Don Larsen's perfect World Series game, a real gem, for less than $125. If you must, buy *one* ceramic statue, but no more; there is little investment potential here.

You can get a couple of Bobbing Head dolls from the 1960s at the same price as one figurine. A Willie Mays mint Bobbing Head goes for $100 +, but most others are reasonably priced. Most of the dolls are not of real players, but cartoonish figures in major league team uniforms. It may change in the future, but as of now, Bobbing Heads don't have much investment potential. But they are some of the most likable collectibles on the market and really brighten a collection.

PEREZ-STEELE CARDS AND HALL OF FAME PLAQUE POSTCARDS

All collectors know of the Perez-Steele cards, large gorgeous baseball cards put out by artist Dick Perez and his partner Frank Steele of Philadelphia. They were printed in three limited sets with 10,000 cards of each star player and have skyrocketed from $153 a set to over $800. Their popularity is due in part to their being an ideal card for players to autograph—they're larger than ordinary cards, and quite beautiful. Unlike baseball cards, Perez-Steele limited-edition cards go up in price when autographed. There are some quite expensive autographed Perez-Steele cards—an autographed Mantle goes for over $200—but most go for $25–50. To buy a set of Perez-Steele cards at the going rate is chancy, because it's unlikely they will go up much higher. But by all means, buy cards of particular favorites or ones you plan to get autographed.

The Hall of Fame Plaque postcards, distributed by the Baseball Hall of Fame in Cooperstown, feature photos of the authentic Hall of Fame plaques. They sell for the price of a postcard but will go up to between $5 and $12 if you get them signed by the Hall of Famer. Such signed souvenirs should probably be worth more, and dealers will try to sell them at outrageous prices—keep your money because you'll have no trouble finding signed HOF Plaques at the going bargain rates or lower. Just keep looking. There's no investment potential here because of mass production, but we like these attractive cards, especially when autographed.

COINS

It has become increasingly common at big card shows to find dealers selling their baseball-player coin collections. You can also order them through the mail from dealers and hobbyists who realize that these coins aren't as much fun to own as you might think, and they aren't in demand. You'll certainly come across the 1955, 1959, and 1960 Armour coins, with players in profile on the front and data on the back. These look like phony coins, the kinds of things you try to slip into pinball or soda machines instead of real coins. Don't buy individual coins unless, of course, your favorite player is on one or you come across an under-priced 1955 Mickey Mantle (the "corrected" name coin is valued at about $125), 1956 Hank Aaron (its $22 price tag is more than double any of the other 19 coins), or the elusive 1960 Bud Daley (which is priced at $500, probably half his monthly salary at the time). But full sets might not be such a bad investment, especially as we move into a new decade and the coins seem older.

The same holds true for the 40-player metal 1965 Old London coins, which you can get for $300–400. The players face forward and the images are clear, so they are more enjoyable and less pretentious than the Armour coins.

The most familiar player coins are the 1962 Salada (Tea) plastic coins. Dealers always drag albums full of these coins to shows and usually drag them home again. A set of more than 200 coins sells for about $4,000—but you'll rarely find anyone who has a full set or wants one. Prices of individual coins vary greatly, without a whole lot of rhyme or reason. Buy your favorite player, buy superstars if you can talk the dealer down to $20 or less (most go for $50), and if the dealer doesn't know what he has, buy low-priced error-variation and limited-run coins of nonstars such as Gary Geiger (valued at $500), Jackie Brandt ($750), Dick Williams ($750), and Eddie Bressoud ($250). It's unlikely you'll find any real bargains at card shows because most dealers are aware of the high prices of certain coins, but the owner of an antique or collectibles store who happens to pick up old baseball coins may think only the famous players are valuable. Keep an eye out.

Salada also put out a 63-player metal coin set in 1963. They are available, but rarely as a full set (which is priced at $275). This set is easier to assemble but has less investment potential than its predecessor, which didn't have much either. But there is something quite delightful about seeing your favorite player on one of these coins, especially if he wasn't a superstar. For instance, you can get coins of Dick Stuart, Turk Farrell, Willie Davis, and others for about $2. Buy such coins if they are your favorite players. Otherwise, just dabble. The same goes for the Topps metal sets issued in 1964 (valued at

$400) and 1971 ($200). We're less excited by the coin sets issued by 7-Eleven in the 1980s, but perhaps they'll have more character when we look at them in twenty years, when the larger sets might be valued at $100 (although that doesn't mean anyone will buy them for that much money). At least youngsters can afford these coins today (and they're preferable to decals and stamps). A better investment may be the yearly sets Topps issues. They may become essential buys for investors, like the Topps card sets; the 1988 Topps coin set may look like it belongs in a bad children's toy department, but it was surprisingly popular and quickly doubled in value.

PINS

Topps pins from 1956, featuring three to five players from each team, are not considered rare, yet they are much harder to find than any of the coin sets. If your favorite player is one of the 60 players, you must buy his pin—it is a wonderful collectible, especially if he's not a star. If he's not a star, you can probably buy his pin for $12–15, if you can find it. Some stars such as Hank Aaron, Willie Mays, and Ted Williams may cost you $00 or more, which is steep, but if you can get them for below $50, you've made a pretty good deal. While price guides suggest lower prices for such pins, the few dealers who have them don't sell them that low. Price guides aren't realistic as far as these pins go—in fact, expect the prices to go up as demand for pins of all kinds increases. Collectors interested in old pins should seek out the Sweet Caporal pins that were produced circa 1910. That set, containing more than 150 players, goes for about $2,500. Don't worry if you're not interested in the entire set. Consider that you can buy many players in that set for less than you'd pay for similar-caliber players in the 1956 Topps set. We don't think they will go up much in value, but at their low prices they're worth taking a chance on. They should go up some as they become rarer— if not now, then certainly in 2010, when they are 100 years old. Anyway, even if you can't resell them today, they are terrific additions to your collection.

By far, the best investments are World Series, All-Star game, and Hall of Fame induction-ceremony press pins. In fact, these hard-to-get items are among the best investments in the entire hobby. Pin mania took a great leap forward during the 1984 Olympics in Los Angeles, when many Americans discovered the athletes' favorite pastime of collecting and trading pins of all nations. There is such a press-pin craze in this country (and abroad) that even though they aren't even baseball fans, many people will want to buy your baseball press pins. You will always be able to sell your press pins—so, obviously, the less you buy them for (perhaps you can get them free or trade for them), the better return you can get. Decade-old press pins routinely sell for a hundred dollars or more. Even World Series, All-Star, and Hall of Fame induction-ceremony press pins from the eighties will approach $100 when we come to 1990. You can take comfort that whatever you buy today will go up tomorrow. This is one item for which even dealers offer high prices. Check out these *buying* prices in a recent hobby newspaper ad placed by the California Numismatic Investments:

1911 Phil World Series: $5,000
1912 Boston W.S.: $1,800
1913 Phil W.S.: $4,200
1919 Chicago W.S.: $3,700
1924 Washington W.S.: $1,250
1934 Detroit W.S.: $525

1938 Cincinnati All-Star: $2,500
1982 HOF: $400
1987 HOF: $400

Because these are buying prices, you know this coin company can sell such pins easily, for much higher prices. So if you have any of these or similar press pins, or know how to get them cheaper, you're in luck. Interestingly, these prices are what dealers charged customers just a year ago. That's how fast these press pins are increasing in value. Even so, you may not want them in a collection because they seem to have so little to do with the game of baseball.

MAGAZINES

The only sports magazines that are worth over $75 are mint issues printed before 1920 or first issues. The inaugural issue of *Sports Illustrated,* containing a special on baseball cards, sells for $125–150, and early twentieth-century issues of *Baseball Magazine* go for $75–90, but those from the thirties and forties are valued at just $25. Even a pre-1900 mint *Sporting News,* which is, granted, a newspaper rather than a magazine, sells for less than $100. (Some from the 1880s go for more than $100.) So obviously if you buy new issues, it will take you many years to make any kind of profit. If you are interested in making a good investment, track down old magazines in thrift shops, comic book stores, and card shows and put together sets. Or find old nonsports magazines with baseball players on the covers. You can sell a sixties *Life* with Mantle on the cover for $35, or a 1930s *Look* with DiMaggio on the cover for $40. (As always, look for New York stars.) That is not a lot of money to the serious investor, but you might be happy with the profit. We say profit because we expect you to buy such items at *very* low prices. You may be able to sell single issues at good prices, but for the most part the best strategy is to put together a large, interesting, diverse collection and sell it all at once. (The buyer will also get the best deal this way, which is something to consider if you want to buy in quantity.) Buy new baseball magazines to *read,* then put them away for many years. The *Street and Smith* baseball annual is always in demand. Buy it and save it.

PENNANTS

Remember all those pennants you used to keep on your wall when you were growing up? Well, take them out of your closets and trunks, because recently they have become valuable collector's items. The reason is clear: other than illustrated game-day posters, no baseball collectible better captures the feeling of a bygone era. So buy and save new pennants, which can be found at ballpark souvenir stands. If you want pennants for other current teams or teams from past decades, you can get them at the bigger card shows or through mail order companies. Some prices:

1925 *Pirates: $400*
1930 *House of David: $450*
1940 *Cubs: $75*
1948 *Pirates: $125*
1949 *Yankees: $125*
1950 *Phillies $300*
1950 *Senators $125*
1954 *Giants: $175*

1956   Reds: $50
1961   Tigers: $50
1964   Giants: $75
1968   Cards World Series: $40
1969   Yankees/Mantle Day: $15
1979   All-Star: $15
1981   Dodgers: $10

The best strategy is to buy pennants of championship teams, popular teams, or teams that no longer exist, such as the Seattle Pilots, Washington Senators, Boston Braves, Milwaukee Braves, St. Louis Browns, Philadelphia Athletics, Brooklyn Dodgers, and New York Giants. If you plan to attend card shows in, say, Pittsburgh and Los Angeles, buy Dodger and Angel pennants in Pittsburgh, where they are cheap because of lack of interest in those teams, and Pittsburgh pennants in Los Angeles. Obviously, if you want to turn a profit to buy other items for your collection, you can unload the L.A.-purchased Pirates material in Pittsburgh, where interest and prices are highest, and the Pittsburgh-purchased Dodger and Angel material in Los Angeles. This is always a smart strategy when buying collectibles and cards.

OTHER MEMORABILIA

Everything connected to baseball, from bat-shaped ballpoint pens to game posters to restaurant matchbooks to *Harper's Weekly* covers to Reggie Bar wrappers is a collectible. There are no standard prices. It's hard to put a value on one-of-a-kind items, so in general those who own them overprice them—and find people willing to meet those prices. If you want a Babe Ruth-signed bat badly enough, you'll gladly pay $3,000 even though it's priced in guides at $2,000—especially if it is never marketed at that lower price. But don't make it a practice to buy at dealers' prices. If you see a *Harper's Weekly* cover listed at $100, don't go spending $300 for it if you come across it at a swank art gallery. Use your head so you don't use your wallet.

Below is a list of exotic memorabilia and their purchase prices at a recent auction. For the most part, these prices represent the market value for these gems:

- *A 10" by 25" color comic newspaper advertising piece, 1930, featuring Babe Ruth ($425)*

- *1947 Brooklyn Dodger yearbook with special Jackie Robinson insert ($200)*

- *A 24" by 32" cardboard advertising broadside announcing a Negro League Championship game—with illustration of Satchel Paige ($2,400)*

- *Babe Ruth 1930s doll ($250)*

- *Yankee press pin from 1955 Japan trip ($500)*

- *Mets lineup cards from the championship season, 1986 ($75)*

- *1973 National League All-Star ring ($600)*

- *Earle Combs's Old-timers Day Longines watch ($1,000)*

- *Babe Ruth store-model child's bat, circa 1930 ($75)*

- *A Yankee stock certificate from 1945 ($150)*

- *Handwritten letter from Walter Johnson to songwriter Harry Ruby in 1942 ($1,600)*

- *Handwritten letter by Connie Mack to president of a minor league in 1938 ($275)*

- *Ticket to Babe Ruth/Ty Cobb charity golf match, autographed by the Babe ($475)*

- *An 1892 letter from eventual Yankee owner Jacob Ruppert and six canceled checks to Hall of Famers ($900)*

- *Program from 1928 dinner honoring the Yankee team, with 30 autographs on it ($1,700)*

- *Five album pages, patched together, containing autographs of 21 1962 Yankees, including Maris, Mantle, and Ford ($50)*

- *Three-dimensional cardboard advertising sign with Ted Williams standing out from it, 10" by 2" by 12" ($250)*

- *Ted Williams Moxie soda rack holder with Williams picture ($165)*

- *Mantle/Maris radio with their pictures on it ($125)*

- *Mantle/Maris T-shirt from 1962 film* Safe at Home *($125)*

- *Mickey bronze statue in bunting position ($98)*

- *Mantle coffee mug (1955) ($122)*

- *Yankee Stadium plastic model kit ($125)*

- *1930s catcher's mask ($50)*

- *1933 World Series press pass for Polo Grounds ($100)*

- *1951 Philadelphia Phillies yearbook ($400)*

- *"Following the Tigers" (yearbook-style book) ($200)*

- *Bob Feller no-hitter-scored game program from 1951 ($51)*

- *Major League Indoor Baseball Game (wood) from 1912 with metal spinner, huge graphic game board, and lineup cards—16 great pictures of then-current stars such as Johnson, Cobb, and Wagner on cover ($1,875)*

- *1955 Dodger autograph book, "The Artful Dodgers," by Tom Meany, with 22 signatures from stars such as Koufax, Snider, and Hodges ($550)*

- *Brooklyn Dodger wood bat pen & pencil set in original box ($550)*

- *Collection of sepia photos that once hung in Ebbets Field Rotunda ($300)*

- *Joe DiMaggio cardboard cigarette lighter holder/display, great picture of Joe D. in color ($400)*

- Pride of the Yankees *film poster, with Gary Cooper as Lou Gehrig ($275)*

- *Yanks charm bracelet, with team name spelled out ($115)*

- *Don Mattingly's high school yearbooks ($120 to $200 each)*

- *Press pass to Giants-Dodgers third and final playoff game in 1951, where Bobby Thomson hit the game-winning home run ($434)*

- *Program from the above game, with Thomson's autograph ($1,000)*

- *Lou Gehrig's 1929 car registration, with beautiful signature of the Iron Horse at bottom ($1,502)*

- *1959 Baltimore Orioles stock certificate ($250)*

- *1889 stock certificate of Philadelphia A's ($275)*

- *1875 Dewitt baseball guide, a bit frayed ($300)*

- *1880s game scorecards ($60 each)*

- *Program for early baseball musical,* The Umpire *($19)*

- *1916 Red Sox program with Ruth listed as pitcher, plus other old-time players listed ($300)*

- *Babe Ruth wristwatch (1920s) in original box ($550)*

- *Boston Red Sox Velvet Tobacco ad, 12" by 19" from 1916 with youthful-looking pitcher Babe Ruth in center. Great colors ($940)*

- *Babe's Musical Bat. A harmonica encased in 4" bat made in 1917 ($160)*

- *Babe Ruth Hartland statue ($175)*

- *One lobby card from* The Babe Ruth Story *lobby-card series ($40)*

- *Huge and sharp photo of the 1902 Chicago White Sox ($2,000)*

- *Three large black-and-white pictures of the 1906 World Series—sharp with lots of crowd scenes ($500 each)*

- *Replica 1919 World Series ring, presented to selected cast members of the movie* Eight Men Out *($1,000)*

- *1919 cardboard World Series ad posters (the Black Sox series) with ballpark and crowd scenes ($250)*

- *Baseball autographed by the eight actors in the 1988*

movie Eight Men Out *who play the eight players thrown out of baseball following the 1919 Black Sox scandal ($200)*

PAY THE LOWEST PRICES

You should buy baseball memorabilia at fair prices. Don't take for granted that the prices you see in an advertisement or on a dealer table at a show are the going rates or even reasonable. The good dealers offer fair prices, even bargains, on memorabilia, while others exploit the ignorance of the consumer and charge prices that are way out of line, especially on autographed merchandise. What should you pay? Well, there is no set price on memorabilia, but we have gone through a year's worth of dealer and reader ads in hobby magazines and monitored card shows and auctions to come up with the following guide. The prices listed are the *lowest* offered that we came across (which doesn't mean you can't find still lower prices). Expect the prices of autographs, autographed photos, autographed balls, and autographed bats to stand pat or go up slightly, but prices of unusual items, especially one-of-a-kind items, could go up a great deal . . . or if there was no interest last year, down this year. Keep in mind that most card shows that feature player autographing sessions include mail order forms in their hobby newspaper and magazine ads. This will allow you to send away for guest-players' autographs on 8 × 10 color photos, Perez-Steele and Hall of Fame plaque cards, and other flat items, balls, and sometimes, bats, but at a slightly higher rate (plus postage) than the promoters charge those who attend the show. Many of the lowest rates that are listed below are what people who attend shows are charged, so if you will order autographed items from a show promoter by mail, remember to add a small amount to each price. When you read your hobby magazines, keep a lookout for major stars appearing at small shows (usually not held in metropolitan areas) because that's when the player charges the promoter a lesser appearance fee and the promoter, in turn, charges the customer less for autographed items. Eventually, almost every major star makes an appearance at one of these small shows, so have patience. Also important: you'll notice that some of the miscellaneous items we've included may seem too highly priced to be considered a bargain—we agree, but we didn't come across anyone offering them at better rates. If a price seems unreasonable to you, trust your instincts.

HANK AARON: *Auto:$6/Auto Photo:$10/Auto Ball:$12/Auto Hall of Fame Plaque:$12/Auto Bat:$79.95/Auto Perez-Steele Card:$40/1956 Topps Pin:$75/1959 Armour Coin:$35/1973 Braves Home Jersey:$2,100/Auto 1976 Braves Home Jersey (worn at Old-Timers Game):$1,500/ Model Mini Bat:$25*

LUIS APARICIO: *Auto Ball:$18*

RICHIE ASHBURN: *Auto:$3/Auto Photo:$6/Auto Ball:$9*

ERNIE BANKS: *Auto:$6/Auto Photo:$8/Auto Ball:$12/Auto Bat:$69/Auto Hall of Fame Plaque:$9/Auto Perez-Steele Card:$25/1956 Topps Pin:$60/1964 Talking Baseball Card:$25*

COOL PAPA BELL: *Auto:$7/Auto Perez-Steele Card:$75/Auto Photo:$15/Auto Ball:$40*

GEORGE BELL: *Auto Ball:$13/Bat:$65/1985 Blue Jays Home Jersey:$895*

JOHNNY BENCH: *Auto:$10/Auto Photo:$12/Auto Ball:$15/ Auto Bat:$70/Auto Wirephoto:$35/Poster Ad for Ked's Shoes:$75/Late 1960s Jersey:$1,100*

YOGI BERRA: *Auto:$6/Auto Photo:$10/Auto Ball:$16/Auto Perez-Steele Card:$40/1951 Comic Book:$30/Hartland Statue:$95*

WADE BOGGS: *Auto:$9/Auto Photo:$11/Auto Ball:$16/Mint Bat:$49.95/Auto Bat:$65/Framed Painting:$150/Auto Figurine:$125/1984 Red Sox Jersey:$1,250*

RALPH BRANCA: *Auto:$4/Auto Photo:$8/Auto Ball:$13*

GEORGE BRETT: *Auto Photo:$10/Auto Ball:$15/Auto Bat:$70/1984 Royals Road Jersey:$900*

LOU BROCK: *Auto:$6/Auto Photo:$8/Auto Ball:$12/Auto Bat:$49/Auto Perez-Steele Card:$25*

ROY CAMPANELLA: *Auto:$45/1950 Comic Book:$30*

JOSE CANSECO: *Auto:$6.50/Auto Photo:$7/Auto Ball:$12/ Auto Bat:$69/Wristband:$30/Auto Game-Used Bat:$300 (Note: After his 1988 MVP season, Canseco was charging between $12 and $15 for an autograph, so expect higher prices on all items listed here.)*

ROD CAREW: *Auto Shoes:$250/Used Bat:$225/1980 Angels Road Jersey:$795*

STEVE CARLTON: *Auto:$8/Auto Photo:$10/Auto Ball:$13.50/ 1984 Bronze Replica:$8*

GARY CARTER: *Auto Baseball Card (for charity): $10/Auto Photo:$12/Mint Bat:$49.95/Auto Bat:$59.95/Auto Cracked Bat:$75/1980 Montreal Road Jersey:$725*

JACK CLARK: *Auto:$7/Auto Photo:$9/Auto Ball:$13/Auto Bat:$55/Cardinals Jersey:$300/Cap:$65/Batting Glove:$30*

WILL CLARK: *Auto:$5.50/Auto Photo:$9/Auto Ball:$15*

ROGER CLEMENS: *Auto:$8/Auto Photo:$12/Auto Ball:$15/ Auto Commemorative Plate:$200*

ROBERTO CLEMENTE: *Bat:$795/Commemorative Plate:$49.50/1988 Figurine:$125/Tankard:$39.95*

TY COBB: *1988 Figurine:$125/Used Bat:$2,000/Cracked Bat:$395*

ERIC DAVIS: *Auto Ball:$13.50/Auto Bat:$55/Wristband:$25/ 1987 Reds Road Jersey:$875*

ANDRE DAWSON: *Auto:$5/Auto Photo:$8/Auto Ball:$12.50/ Wristband:$25/Commemorative Plate:$49.50/Auto Figurine:$125/1984 Expos Batting Helmet:$175/Auto Gold Plate:$125*

DIZZY DEAN: *Auto:$45/Auto B&W Photo:$75/1930s Cardinals Jersey:$2,500–4,000*

LOU DIALS: *Auto:$3/Auto Photo:$6/Auto Ball:$9*

BILL DICKEY: *Auto Photo:$15/Auto Ball:$30/Auto Hall of Fame Plaque:$13/Auto Perez-Steele Card:$90/Mitt:$3,000*

JOE DIMAGGIO: *Auto:$15/Auto Photo:$19/Auto Ball:$40/ Auto Perez-Steele Card:$225/Unsigned Plate:$100/Silk Cachets Commemorating 50th Anniversary of Debut:$29.95/Cigarette Lighter-Holder Ad:$495*

LARRY DOBY: *Auto Photo:$6/1950 Comic Book:$10/1955 Armour Coin:$9*

BOBBY DOERR: *Auto:$3/Auto Photo:$6/Auto Ball:$9/Auto Perez-Steele Card:$30/Auto Hall of Fame Plaque:$30*

DON DRYSDALE: *Auto:$7/Auto Photo:$10/Auto Ball:$15/ Auto Hall of Fame Plaque:$9/Auto Perez-Steele Card:$30/ 1956 Brooklyn Dodger Payroll Check:$500/1960 Armour Coin:$30/1958 L.A. Dodger Road Jersey:$3,500/1964 Talking Baseball Card:$25*

BOB FELLER: *Auto:$4/Auto Photo:$6/Auto Ball:$8/Auto Perez-Steele Card:$30/Jersey:$750*

ROLLIE FINGERS: *Auto:$4/Auto Photo:$6/Auto Ball:$10/1984 Bronze Replica:$7*

WHITEY FORD: *Auto $7/Auto Photo:$9/Auto Ball:$14/Auto Perez-Steele Card:$35/1960 Armour Coin:$30/1964 Talking Baseball Card:$25*

STEVE GARVEY: *Auto:$8/Auto Photo:$11/Auto Ball:$12.50/ Auto Bat:$135/1974–75 Dodger MVP Trophy:$1,595/1981 Dodger Road Jersey:$900*

LOU GEHRIG: *Auto:$550/Auto Photo:$300+/Auto Ball:$1,000/Signed Car Registration:$1,502/Ad in 1935 Colliers for Camel Cigarettes:$12/Commemorative Plate:$45/ 1988 Figurine:$125*

BOB GIBSON: *Auto:$6/Auto Photo:$6/Auto 1969 Postcard:$15/Auto Ball:$13/Auto Hall of Fame Ball:$25/Auto Perez-Steele Card:$30*

KIRK GIBSON: *Auto Photo:$6/Auto Ball:$10/Auto Bat:$49/ 1985 Tigers Road Jersey:$500*

LEFTY GOMEZ: *Auto:$6/Auto Ball:$15/Auto Hall of Fame Plaque:$9/Auto Perez-Steele Card:$70*

DWIGHT GOODEN: *Auto:$8/Auto Photo:$10/Auto Ball:$13/ Auto Bat:$85/Auto Framed Painting:$200/Beach Towel:$20/1986 Mets Home Jersey:$975/Glove:$1,000*

HANK GREENBERG: *Auto Ball:$75/Auto Perez-Steele Card:$325*

MIKE GREENWELL: *Auto:$6/Auto Photo:$9/Auto Ball:$12*

TONY GWYNN: *Auto:$6/Auto Photo:$8/Auto Ball:$12.50/Auto Bat:$65*

RICKEY HENDERSON: *Auto Photo:$10/Auto Ball:$20/Auto Bat:$65/1981 A's Home Jersey:$875*

KEITH HERNANDEZ: *Auto Photo:$9.50/Auto Ball:$15/Auto Bat:$60*

CARL HUBBELL: *Auto Photo:$12/Auto Ball:$12/Auto Hall of Fame Plaque:$12/Auto All-Star Strikeout-Feat Cachet:$40*

JIM HUNTER: *Auto:$6/Auto Photo:$9/Auto Ball:$17.50/Auto Perez-Steele Card:$25/1973 A's Jersey:$975*

MONTE IRVIN: *Auto:$6/Auto Photo:$5/Auto Ball:$12/Auto Hall of Fame Plaque:$7*

REGGIE JACKSON: *Auto:$15/Auto Photo:$16/Auto Ball:$30/ Auto Bat:$100/Cracked Bat:$175/1973 Used Glove:$550/ Auto Commemorative Plate:$150/Unsigned Commemorative Plate:$75/1984 Bronze Replica:$7/1973 A's Jersey:$975/1976 Orioles Jersey:$1,495*

GREGG JEFFERIES: *Auto:$10/Auto Photo:$7/Auto Ball:$15*

WALLY JOYNER: *Auto Photo:$6/Auto Ball:$11/Auto Bat:$50/ Auto Commemorative Plate:$150/Unsigned Commemorative Plate:$60/Auto Game-Used Bat:$100*

AL KALINE: *Auto:$5/Auto Photo:$8/Auto Ball:$13/Auto Game-Used Bat:$360/Auto Hall of Fame Plaque:$8/Auto Perez-Steele Card:$30/1960 Armour Coin:$30/1988 Figurine:$125/1964 Talking Baseball Card:$20*

GEORGE KELL: *Auto:$4/Auto Photo:$5/Auto Ball:$9/Auto Perez-Steele Card:$30*

HARMON KILLEBREW: *Auto:$5/Auto Photo:$5/Auto Ball:$8/ Auto Hall of Fame Plaque:$6/Auto Perez-Steele Card:$17.50/Auto Bat:$49/1974 Twins Home Jersey:$1,100*

RALPH KINER: *Auto:$5/Auto Photo:$9/Auto Bat:$65/Auto Perez-Steele Card:$30/1950 Comic Book:$10*

SANDY KOUFAX: *Auto:$11/Auto Photo:$12.50/Auto Ball:$18/ Auto Perez-Steele Card:$50/Auto Commemorative Plate:$250/1956 Brooklyn Dodgers Payroll Check:$600/ 1964 Talking Baseball Card:$30*

AL LEITER: *Auto Ball:$15*

BOB LEMON: *Auto Ball:$18.95/Auto Perez-Steele Card:$30*

BUCK LEONARD: *Auto:$8/Auto Photo:$10*

WILLIE MCCOVEY: *Auto Ball:$16.95/Auto Perez-Steele Card:$25*

MARK MCGWIRE: *Auto:$7/Auto Photo:$10/Auto Ball:$15/ Auto Bat:$69/Auto Used Bat:$150/B&W Tacoma Photo:$8/ 1987 A's Jersey:$1,995/Auto Cletes:$325/Batting Glove Auto:$75/1988 Figurine:$125*

DENNY MCLAIN: *Auto:$4/Auto Photo:$3.50/Auto Ball:$10*

MICKEY MANTLE: *Auto:$12/Auto Photo:$19/Auto Ball:$35/ Auto Perez-Steele Card:$215/Auto 1988 Figurine:$125+/ Mint Bat:$79.95/Auto Bat:$99/Auto Black Bat:$385/Com- memorative Plate Auto:$250/Unsigned Plate:$150/Litho- graph:$375/1955 Coffee Mug:$122/Bronze Statue in Bunting Position:$98/1964 Talking Baseball Cards:$75*

JUAN MARICHAL: *Auto:$6/Auto Photo:$8/Auto Ball:$12/ Poster:$10*

ROGER MARIS: *Auto:$75/Auto Reversed Photo of 60th Homer:$225/Auto Ball:$100/1964 Talking Baseball Card:$30*

MIKE MARSHALL: *Cletes:$35/Wristband:$10/Batting Gloves:$25/1984 Home Jersey:$325*

BILLY MARTIN: *Auto:$6/Auto Photo:$10/Auto Ball:$12/Auto Bat:$75*

EDDIE MATHEWS: *Auto:$4/Auto Photo:$6/Auto Ball:$12/ Auto Hall of Fame Plaque:$7/Auto Bat:$65/Auto Perez-Steele Card:$30/1960 Armour Coin:$30*

DON MATTINGLY: *Auto Ball:$25/Mint Bat:$40/Auto Matted Photo:$44/"Hit Man" Poster:$9/Baseball Card Kit:$10/1988 Figurine:$225/1984 Yankee Road Uniform:$1,850/High School Yearbook:$120*

WILLIE MAYS: *Auto:$8.50/Auto Photo:$11/Auto Ball/$15/ Auto Bat:$69/Auto Perez-Steele Card:$75/Bobbing Head:$100+/Auto Commemorative Plate:$250/1960 Armour Coin:$30*

JOHNNY MIZE: *Auto:$3/Auto Photo:$4/Auto Ball:$9/Auto Hall of Fame Plaques:$7/Auto Perez-Steele Card:$30*

THURMAN MUNSON: *Game-Used Bat:$522.50*

DALE MURPHY: *Auto Photo:$10/Auto Bat:$65/1979 Atlanta Road Jersey:$975/Poster Ad for Champion Spark Plugs:$25*

EDDIE MURRAY: *Auto Ball:$18/Mint Bat:$75/Wrist Band:$18/1987 Orioles Road Jersey:$875*

STAN MUSIAL: *Auto:$8/Auto Photo:$8/Auto Ball:$14/Auto Bat:$69/Auto Perez-Steele Card:$75*

MATT NOKES: *Auto:$4/Auto Photo:$9/Auto Ball:$13*

SATCHEL PAIGE: *Auto:$30/Auto Perez-Steele Card:$295/St. Louis Browns Pin:$15/1935 Negro League Baseball Poster:$2,650*

JIM PALMER: *Auto:$7/Auto Photo:$10/Auto Ball:$13/1977 Orioles Road Jersey:$1,000*

GAYLORD PERRY: *Auto:$5/Auto Photo:$4/Auto Ball:$9/1982 Mariners Home Jersey:$850*

JOHNNY PODRES: *Auto:$3/Auto Photo:$6.95/Auto Ball:$12.95*

KIRBY PUCKETT: *Auto:$6/Auto Photo:$6/Auto Ball:$10/Auto Bat:$49*

TIM RAINES: *Cracked Bat:$85/1984 Expos Jersey:$995*

PEE WEE REESE: *Auto Ball:$30/Auto Perez-Steele Card:$30/ 1955 Armour Coin:$30/1950s Dodger Jersey:$4,000*

JIM RICE: *Bat:$60/1980 Red Sox Home Jersey:$595*

CAL RIPKEN, JR.: *Auto Ball:$15.95/Auto Uncracked Bat:$110/Cracked Bat:$85/1985 Orioles Road Jersey:$900*

PHIL RIZZUTO: *Auto Ball:$10/1951 Comic Book:$20*

ROBIN ROBERTS: *Auto:$4/Auto Photo:$8/Auto Ball:$12/Auto Hall of Fame Plaque:$15/Auto Perez-Steele Card:$30/1954 Model Glove:$75*

BROOKS ROBINSON: *Auto:$4/Auto Photo:$7/Auto Ball:$11/ Auto Perez-Steele Card:$15/Auto Bat:$49*

FRANK ROBINSON: *Auto:$8/Auto Photo:$9/Auto Ball:$16/ Auto Perez-Steele Card:$30/Auto Bat:$75/1973 Home Angels Jersey:$800/1959 Armour Coins:$25/1964 Talking Baseball Card:$25*

JACKIE ROBINSON: *Auto with Perez-Steele Card:$395/Auto Ball:$135+/Bat Mint Model:$79.95/1949–50 Comic Book:$50/1956 Topps Pin:$65/1949 Doll:$875/Auto Dollar Bill:$310/1982 Hall of Fame Program:$40*

PETE ROSE: *Auto:$9/Auto Photo:$10/Auto Ball:$14/Auto Bat:$85/Auto Black Bat:$500/Auto Painting:$1,500/Auto Commemorative Plate:$200/Unsigned Commemorative Plate:$75/Auto 1988 Figurine:$350/1983 Phillies Home Jersey:$995/1983 Montreal Warm-up Jersey:$500/Cachet Commemorating 4,000th Hit:$75/Glove:$1,000/Auto Phillies Cap:$300*

BABE RUTH: *Auto:$550/Auto with Perez-Steele Card:$1,200/ Auto Photo:$800/Auto Ball:$800/Auto Game-Used Bat:$2,000/Commemorative Plate:$45/1988 Figurine:$125/ Auto Store-Bought Bat:$1,100/Used Bat:$1,200/Signed Personal Check:$1,500/1930s Doll:$250/1930s Child's Model Bat:$75/1920s Wristwatch in Box:$550/Hartland Statue:$175/Sheet Music ("Babe Ruth! Babe Ruth!"):$65*

NOLAN RYAN: *Auto Photo:$10/Auto Ball:$15/1970s Angels Road Jersey:$950*

BRET SABERHAGEN: *Auto Photo:$5/Auto Ball:$10/Auto Bat:$69/1984 Royals Road Jersey:$475*

BENITO SANTIAGO: *Auto:$5.50/Auto Photo:$5/Auto Ball:$10*

MIKE SCHMIDT: *Auto Ball:$15/Auto Bat:$100/Auto Game-Used Bat:$150/Auto Batting Glove:$10/Auto Spikes:$125*

TOM SEAVER: *Auto:$10/Auto Ball:$19.95/Auto Commemorative Plate:$200/Unsigned Commemorative Plate:$75/Auto Lithograph of 300th Win:$50/1977 Reds Road Jersey:$995*

KEVIN SEITZER: *Auto Photo:$5/Auto Ball:$9/Auto Bat:$69*

ENOS SLAUGHTER: *Auto:$4/Auto Photo:$7/Auto Ball:$9/ Auto Bat:$60/Auto Hall of Fame Plaque:$7/Auto Perez-Steele Postcard:$30*

OZZIE SMITH: *Auto Photo:$6.50/Auto Ball:$12/Auto Bat:$200/Wristband:$15*

DUKE SNIDER: *Auto:$4/Auto Photo:$6.50/Auto Ball:$12/ Auto Bat:$49/Auto Perez-Steele Card:$30/1955 Armour Coin:$35/Auto 1955 Jersey:$5,000/1950 Model Glove:$75*

WARREN SPAHN: *Auto:$4/Auto Photo:$6/Auto Ball:$11/Auto Hall of Fame Plaque:$10/Auto Perez-Steele Card:$30/1955 Armour Coin:$30/1956 Topps Pin:$50/Jersey:$2,000/1964 Talking Baseball Card:$25*

WILLIE STARGELL: *Auto:$6/Auto Photo:$6/Auto Ball:$18/ Auto Bat:$49*

DAVE STEWART: *Auto:$4.50/Auto Photo:$4/Auto Ball:$9*

DARRYL STRAWBERRY: *Auto:$8/Auto Photo:$10/Auto Ball:$14/Wristband:$25/1984 Mets Home Jersey:$1,200/ Auto Game-Used Bat:$125*

BILL TERRY: *Auto Photo:$12/Auto Ball:$18/Auto Bat:$125/ Auto Game-Used Cracked Bat:$300/Auto Hall of Fame Plaque:$12/Auto Perez-Steele Card:$90*

BOBBY THOMSON: *Auto:$4/Auto Photo:$8/Auto Ball:$13*

LUIS TIANT: *Auto:$3.50/Auto Photo:$6.50/Auto Ball:$10/Red Sox Jersey:$350*

FERNANDO VALENZUELA: *Auto Ball:$15/1983 Dodgers Jersey:$600*

BILLY WILLIAMS: *Auto:$4/Auto Photo:$8/Auto Ball:$13/Auto Perez-Steele Card:$25*

TED WILLIAMS: *Auto:$15/Auto Photo:$20/Auto Ball:$30/ Auto Bat:$100/Auto Hall of Fame Plaque:$55/Auto Figurine:$125/Auto Perez-Steele Card:$125/Auto Fenway Park Postcard:$25/Auto Plate:$125/1950 B&W Pin:$10/Window Sticker Ad for Moxie Soda:$1,100*

DAVE WINFIELD: *Auto Photo:$10/Auto Ball:$15/Auto Bat:$75/Auto Autobiography:$16.95/1979 Padres Home Jersey:$850*

CARL YASTRZEMSKI: *Auto:$8/Auto Photo:$10/Auto Ball:$15/ Auto Bat:$75/1975 Red Sox Road Jersey:$1,250/1979 Home Red Sox Jersey:$975*

OTHER MISCELLANEOUS PLAYER MATERIAL

Walter Johnson Handwritten Letter to Harry Ruby: $1,600
Honus Wagner Cracked Bat: $700
Rogers Hornsby Used Bat: $1,500
Luke Appling Auto: $5
Ed Roebuck Dodgers Payroll Check: $100
Elston Howard Yankees Jersey: $550
Joe Garagiola Auto Ball: $15
Nap Lajoie Game-Used Bat:$2,000
Tommy Henrich Auto: $5
Dave Steib Blue Jays Jersey: $950
Mark Fidrych Tigers Jersey: $500
Minnie Minoso White Sox Jersey: $500
Smoky Joe Wood Personal Check: $20

Smoky Joe Wood Auto: $15
Pie Traynor Auto: $35
Eddie Cicotte Auto Ball: $35
Muhammad Ali Auto Ball: $35
Sadaharu Oh Auto Photo: $30
Shoeless Joe Jackson Auto Ball: $0 (it's a forgery—he signed with an "X")
Al Simmons Auto Cracked Bat: $400
Bill Madlock Auto Cracked Bat: $45

MISCELLANEOUS MULTIPLAYER MATERIAL

(Notice that usually when a star player adds his signature to an item that has already been autographed by an equal star, the item's value merely doubles (if that) in value. Only when full or nearly full teams sign an item does its value increase significantly.)

Mickey Mantle–Roger Maris Radio (with their picture): $125
Babe Ruth–Lou Gehrig Auto Ball: $1,500
Babe Ruth–several other players Auto Ball: $1,000 +
Babe Ruth–several Hall of Famers Auto Ball: $1,300 +
Several All–Stars Auto Ball: $200 +
Warren Spahn–Ed Mathews Auto Ball: $30
Bobby Thomson–Ralph Branca Auto Photo: $12/Auto Ball: $20
Mickey Mantle–Roger Maris *Safe at Home* Lobby Card: $65
Mickey Mantle–Roger Maris *Safe at Home* T-shirt: $125
Don Mattingly–George Brett–Wade Boggs Auto Photo: $35
Bo Jackson–George Brett Auto Photo: $16
Mickey Mantle–Pete Rose Auto Photo: $35
Don Mattingly–Rickey Henderson–Dave Winfield Auto Photo: $30

Eric Davis–Kal Daniels–Dave Parker Auto Photo: $16
Don Mattingly–Mickey Mantle "Yankee Tradition" Plate:
  $49.50
Reggie Jackson–Don Mattingly Auto Photo: $26
Babe Ruth–George Earnshaw–Al Simmons Auto Ball: $800
Enos Slaughter–Ralph Kiner–Lou Brock Auto Ball: $65
Jose Canseco–Reggie Jackson–Mark McGwire Auto Photo:
  $30
Eric Davis–Darryl Strawberry Auto Photo: $17
Tony Perez–Joe Morgan–Johnny Bench–Pete Rose Auto
  Photo: $35
Pete Rose–Wade Boggs Auto Photo: $19
Mickey Mantle–Ted Williams Auto Ball: $100

CHAPTER 4

PUTTING TOGETHER Y·O·U·R COLLECTION

In the two previous chapters, we offered advice on how to put together a baseball card collection and how to put together a collection of memorabilia, whether you were interested in just a certain type of memorabilia or all types. Now we'd like to help you smartly put together a nice mix of cards and memorabilia, which in our opinion is the ideal baseball collection.

The key to building a nice collection at minimal cost is to find investment-quality items you want at prices you are happy to pay. There's no point in spending $300 on cards in a shop or on memorabilia at a show if you can get the same merchandise for less than $100 and have more fun doing it. All it takes is a little hard work, some basic strategy and knowledge of the best places to get particular items, and a sense of adventure. You've got to be willing to move around and tap different sources for the best deals on cards and collectibles.

As we urged earlier, search your own closets, attics, drawers, trunks, bookshelves, magazine collections, basements, etc., and see what you can turn up. Then, if you still have access to it, search the house or apartment where you grew up. Ask your mother or father if they remember what happened to certain items from your youth. On rare occasions, they didn't throw something out but gave it to a younger cousin or next-door neighbor; it's time to reclaim your treasure. Ask relatives, friends, office workers, and neighbors if they have old cards or collectibles they don't want or are willing to sell. Prized items do turn up this way.

Instead of going straight to a card shop or show in hopes of selling the discovered treasure, novice collectors will get better deals and more satisfaction if they trade with each other. Trading is a wonderful avenue for people starting collections. You can trade your own doubles or triples for cards you need to complete sets of your favorite team, star sets, or full sets. Your neighbor or friend at the office may be looking for 1988 Phillies cards. Being a Cardinals fan who couldn't care less about Philadelphia, you will gladly give him the Phillies he wants (especially your doubles) for the Cards you need. No money changes hands and both collectors are happy. With memorabilia, deals should be transacted carefully, with both parties knowledgeable about the value of the discussed items. It's often easiest and least scary to trade similar items, with the only variable being the different players or teams.

You can meet collectors anywhere—the office, school, the

local card shop, the golf course. You can get together with people you met at a show and work out marvelous deals. You'll always hear a collector trying to sell something to a dealer, only to be offered too low a price. You can step in and buy his item for a price between what he wants for it and what the dealer is willing to pay. Similarly, other collectors will offer you deals when they hear you unsuccessfully bargaining with a dealer. This is your opportunity to make a satisfactory deal and find a good trading buddy.

For novices and kids especially, trading is a good way to get cards and inexpensive collectibles without money being a factor. There is a limit, however, to how much trading two collectors can do. Each is restricted by the size of his own collection and a reluctance to part with what he's collected. Serious collectors have to explore the major outlets for cards and memorabilia. Of course, go to the ballpark on giveaway nights and buy inexpensive team and star-player items at the souvenir stand. And search thrift shops, especially for magazines. But you should also learn what the other major outlets are likely to have and the strategies to follow to get the best deals.

ANTIQUE STORES

With their old green-and-white awnings, columned porches, and slightly disheveled looks, antique stores are as American as baseball itself—and a wonderful place to find old sports memorabilia. The antique store, more than any other spot, is where the great "treasure hunt" for memorabilia should begin. Baseball memorabilia, be it an old bat, a magazine cover, or a photo from 1922, is not easy to find unless you want to be dull and dreary and walk into a card show to buy it. It's the hunt that's exciting, that takes you wandering through small towns and big cities, trodding country lanes and city alleys in search of ballpark treasures.

Sports memorabilia is rare, and that's what makes it valuable to you and not to an antique store. An antique store owner's business is furniture, lamps, china, jewelry, rugs. To him or her, an old picture of Babe Ruth is just another old picture, an old bat from 1922 is just another old piece of wood, a 1935 *Who's Who in the Major Leagues* just another old book. They price them cheaply. Antique stores are full of good finds. Examples of recent finds: a *Who's Who* book, worth $80, sold at $10; an old candy-store baseball scoreboard, worth $50, sold at $12; an old Tom Seaver magazine cover in frame, worth $20, sold at $5; a 1912 photo of the Philadelphia A's, worth $200, sold at $30.

Stroll into the antique store casually and look around first. Never, never, act eager. If there is sports memorabilia, offhandedly ask the price and whatever it is, cringe. He'll come down. Sports memorabilia does not sell for these people and they usually want to unload it. You'll get a discount. Always, always ask if there is more or if he has any in the back room. He often does.

When you leave an antique store, give the owner your name, address, and telephone number; ask him to call you if anything comes in or if he spots anything in his searches. This works. One time an antique dealer called us two months after we saw him and said he had an old glove. We walked in the next day and picked up this beauty, a 1930 first baseman's mitt worth over $75, for just $10.

Antique dealers, knowing you want baseball items, will even shop for you. One, with a steady sports customer, picked up several items at a garage sale for him. The dealer paid $30 and charged his sports customer $60. The items were

worth over $300 in the sports memorabilia market. Was any-
one cheated? Of course not. The garage-sale owner made $30
more than he thought he would; the dealer made a 100 percent profit.

And browsing through antique stores, or antique areas, can
be a nice day in the country and lots of fun. We frequently
browse through stores in Chester, New Jersey, one of the
nation's top antique store meccas. The woman who runs the
Painted Pony there sells many sports items and holds some
aside for us because we're regulars. We go from store to store
once a month and become friendly with the store owners. It's
fun.

COLLECTIBLES STORES

Collectibles stores are much less intimidating than antique
stores. They are "hip" establishments that sell campy,
kitschy, and fun material that represent aspects of twentieth-
century American culture—such as music, film, television,
theater, and sports, particularly America's national pastime.
You're most likely to find souvenir plates, pennants, buttons,
pins, toys and games, figurines, photographs (but not many),
press pins, sheet music, tickets, magazines, and novelty
items. You will occasionally find a stack or two of old baseball
cards mixed in with other cards from the fifties and sixties.
Low-valued cards tend to be slightly overpriced, but there
may be a big plus: all cards in the stack, even of stars, may
have the same price. There is always the chance, especially
in small, isolated towns, that you can get a very rare, expensive card at a very low price because the collectibles store
owner doesn't distinguish between stars and common players
in particular sets. If the store has a savvy owner, don't expect

to pick up great bargains on either cards or memorabilia. Still, you may come across an item you won't see anywhere else, which you can buy at an acceptable price and then, without guilt, sell at a higher price because its rareness justifies its escalating value. You won't get away with acting as naive as you can pretend to be in an antique store, but to get the lowest possible price, still indicate that you are interested in an item because you feel nostalgic or want to buy someone a fun present. Never act excited when you come across a valuable card or rare collectible, and never act as if you have a lot of money to spend. Yes, we realize this is obvious advice, but some overly exuberant collectors definitely need it.

FLEA MARKETS AND GARAGE SALES

An increasing amount of baseball material has been turning up at flea markets in the last two or three years. They're good places to treasure hunt because you'll eventually come across all types of memorabilia and old and new cards. You'll have an easier time finding bargains on memorabilia from people who are cleaning out their houses or, if they make a living selling goods at flea markets, unloading all the material they purchased on their most recent buying tour. They may have bought someone's entire inventory, including miscellaneous baseball material they know nothing about and don't know how to price. Use the same naive technique you would use in an antique store, but be more chatty and friendly. You're not out to gyp these people, just get a bargain. There's a good chance you can talk dealers at flea markets into lowering their prices if you are friendly and show an instant liking for a particular item.

It used to be that you could count on getting good deals on

baseball cards at flea markets. Cards used to be scattered on tables because no one cared what happened to them. After all, they were just the kid's worthless cards from the previous year and he was now more interested in this year's cards. But today, the kid is there with his parents and is personally hawking his cards, which are carefully kept in a snazzy album. Instead of offering bargain deals, these kids overprice their cards. For all 3¢ common-player cards, the kid will charge 25¢; for any other nonstar or rookie player, he'll charge $1, and he won't even offer any of his stars or rookies. They correctly figure that no one will bring a price guide to a flea market. These kids have learned well . . . from their fathers, who stand next to their sons and daughters with their albums of overpriced older cards.

But keep trying, because at flea markets some people who do know the correct values of cards and memorabilia will offer discounts. That's because many are dealing in great volume. At one flea market we attended, a baseball card shop owner was selling stacks of 40 to 50 older cards for about $50. Sold individually, the cards were worth over $130. Why was he doing this? He found that he could unload them on a busy Sunday afternoon to the general public faster than he could on five business days at his store to only hard-core collectors. Dealers are willing to be more flexible at flea markets. For the collector, this means great bargains.

Garage sales, so popular in California, are a good place to get good bargains, especially on cards. Garage sales are usually held by one or two families, neighbors, and take place on the lawn, in the driveway, in the garage, and possibly in the house itself. Kids tend to wander away because they're at home, leaving their mothers to mind their cards. If you have the heart for it (or don't have a heart at all), snap up those cards before the kid returns. You may also have the opportunity to buy the husband's old glove or bat, which his wife took out of the garage to sell, assuming it was just more of her kid's newer baseball items. If you spot a baseball item not for sale, ask about it anyway, and you may soon own it at a good price. Anyway, even if the husband were there, he might test the waters with his prized baseball possessions, especially if he doesn't have to drag it to a flea market to sell it. It's not unusual for men to become curious about what they will be offered for their prized item, and they are usually impressed by the figure you come up with. Many collectors spend entire Saturdays, week after week, searching garage sales for buried treasure. Some find it. One elderly woman, eager to move to Florida, wanted to sell everything in her house at a garage sale. A collector asked about baseball cards. She brought down a box. "They're my son's. Tell you what, a quarter each." In the box was a Mike Schmidt rookie card and other gems. For $16, the collector bought about $400 worth of cards. And the woman was delighted to get rid of them and make an unexpected $16.

THE CARD SHOP

The card shop is the candy store of the baseball card world. A new phenomenon a few years ago, the baseball card shop has now become a staple of the hobby and the community. There are now over 3,500 card shops in the country, and in some areas, such as northern New Jersey, a single county may have as many as ten shops within a fifteen-minute drive of one another. There are different kinds of shops: the pure baseball card shop, where the only things for sale are cards and sports memorabilia; the combination sporting goods and card shop where, in addition to cards, you can buy sneakers,

T-shirts, and some sports equipment; and the cards and comics shop, where the store is half cards, half comics.

The card shop can be a good place to buy and sell cards, and to a lesser degree, collectibles. It all depends on how you utilize your local card shop and get along with its owner. He is like any other store owner; he can be standoffish to strangers and warm to friends and steady customers. He is much like the guy in the old candy store who'd let you have a free soda if you didn't have enough change after school. Now, he lets you have the $5 card for the $4 in quarters in your pocket, or gives you the old beat-up cards he figures he can't sell, or throws in an inexpensive collectible if you make a purchase.

Prices in card shops tend to be a bit higher than prices at shows, particularly on bigger items such as card sets, '50s star cards, and albums. A $6 album at a card show is generally $8 or more at a card shop. A $15 McGwire rookie card at a show is generally $20 or more at a card shop. This is not a rip-off. This is the price of the card shop's overhead—rent, heat, employees, taxes, advertising, and promotion.

However, you can establish a relationship with a card store owner you never get with a dealer at a show, whom you may never see again. A card shop owner wants you for a steady customer—*needs* you for a steady customer. He makes money only if he has a steady market for his cards and memorabilia, and happy customers are frequent customers.

You can expect the good card shop owner to fill your needs. If you desire a Mickey Mantle 1955 Bowman in moderately priced very good condition, he can get it for you, either taking it from the store's inventory, pulling it from his own private collection, or putting the word out among other collectors and dealers. If you're looking for a particular piece of memorabilia—Tigers ticket stubs, elusive 1956 Topps pins, a low-priced DiMaggio-autographed ball—he'll join the search. If you don't see certain memorabilia in a store, still ask about it because the owner may have memorabilia in a locked store-room, have his own collection (which is very likely), or have easy access to memorabilia collectors and dealers. He'll save you the hassle of driving to four different shows in four different counties to get what you want. He has friends and contacts. He has access to the card companies that his customers don't have. He can guarantee you the elusive Fleer set each year. He can guarantee you the peculiar card set you read about but can't find (and probably shouldn't buy anyway). He'll be happy to order cards and memorabilia for you. He can also give you good discounts if you buy in bulk. And the good card shop owner pays equal attention to kids, although they have less money to spend than adults. If you are a good, steady customer, ask for good deals on merchandise. You are entitled. The good shop owner wants you as much as you want him.

Colin Koeck, who owns The Coinery, a card and coin shop in the Rockaway Mall, in Rockaway, New Jersey, has a typical view of the profession: "A baseball card shop is like any other store in the community. I make my money on solid relationships with hundreds of customers who come back week after week—just like a candy store or hardware store or supermarket. If I don't provide good service and take care of peoples' needs, they'll go elsewhere. My job is get people what they want at reasonable prices. The fun in a card shop, though, is that it's baseball we're dealing with—so people want to talk and tell stories and swap tales about cards. It's enjoyable. That's why I do it."

AUCTIONS

Everyone has heard of card auctions. Are they worth a visit, or if a publication auction, a phone call or letter bid?

Yes, if you are looking to spend a lot of money and have several hours to browse through items to be auctioned and to sit through the endless bidding in order to get what you want. They are especially worth it if you can snag items going at real bargain prices.

To get bargains, though, you will sit through about three hours of tedious talking and bidding, and then you'll have to outbid an audience comprised mostly of dealers. You can do well, though, if you're lucky. At one recent auction a man got an incredible bargain, $600 worth of cards for $150, because the three dealers interested in the lot of cards had run out of money by the time the item came up. At other times, you can make out well if you are there to bid on a specific item. If no one else is interested in that item, and this is often the case, you can land it cheaply. And at an auction, almost every one has a group of boxes filled with between 1,000 and 10,000 cards that go for $40 or less.

However, be warned that these auctions are conducted by dealers for dealers. You sit there with your $65 hoping for a buy on something you may like, but there are ten dealers sitting near you with $5,000; you are not going to outbid them if they want your item. You could sit there all night and lose every single bid.

Mail and phone auctions are different, and a much better arrangement for the small collector. For these, circle items listed in ads in trade publications and mail or phone in a bid. If it's close enough to what the dealer has in mind and there have been few mail or phone bids, your chance of landing the item is great. We recently heard of someone who bid a miserly $5 for a 1915 advertising poster with a market value of $50. Over 50,000 people read the ad, which listed 150 auction items, but not one other person made a bid on the poster. Our man with his $5 gamble won it. There are hundreds of cases of low-ball bidders getting $20 autographed baseballs, a popular item, for $10 or less.

An advantage of the mail and phone auction is that you don't have to sit through bidding for dozens of items you don't want to get to one you do. You also get to go right to the price you're willing to pay. You may of course be outbid, even outbid by phone at the very last minute, but your chance of getting an item via phone or mail are pretty good. Remember, the person auctioning the items can decline to sell them if the bids are too low. However, he will call you and say your $10 bid on his $100 item is being turned down and give you a chance to meet the price he'll settle for, say, $30.

Auction items usually have a minimum bid figure, and that's the seller's bottom-line price. Some items, however, particularly expensive ones, have no minimum bid, and low-ball bidders won't get their bargains. The seller of a Ruth ball worth $1,000 will simply turn down bids under $300— and justifiably so. However, then you know his bottom-line figure and if you want, can go to $300, which is still a good deal on that item.

The downside to mail and auction bidding is that you have no idea who is bidding what for your item. You may think you have a $600 Gehrig autograph locked up only to lose it on a last-minute phone call bid of $650 from California. Overall, though, auctions can give you reasonably good bargains. Just don't assume you're going to outbid dealers, the pros.

MAIL ORDER

"We're a source of information, a dispenser of news, and a marketplace where people can buy and sell things with some direction from us," says Bob Lemke, publisher of *Sports Collectors Digest*. *SCD* and the other hobby magazines are loaded with huge ads by dealers and hobbyists from all over America. Should you buy from these people? Do they offer good buys? Are strangers who live 2,000 miles away reliable?

There are dealers and hobbyists whose ads for box specialty sets, commons, reprint sets, and other worthless cards make their products sound like the best investments around. There are dealers and hobbyists who have the nerve to say they possess the finest Play Ball 1940 set or Ted Williams 1954 Bowman or Topps 1956 set they have ever had the privilege of seeing—and although they'll admit few of the star cards are in mint condition, they'll be willing to sell their treasure to you if you pay even more than the mint-condition prices listed in the magazine containing the ad. (Coin stores are notorious for pricing their products higher than the prices listed by the hobby magazines.) And there are hobbyists 2,000 miles away who will take your money and promptly forget all about their part of the transaction.

But for the most part, dealers and hobbyists are honest and reliable and their mail order prices are a bit below book and very competitive with shows and stores. Dealers will mail you cards in safe boxes to prevent bending or handling, will insure cards and memorabilia upon request, and will refund money if you didn't receive what you expected. They will also be willing to talk to you about your purchase and advise you on future transactions. *SCD* and other hobby magazines will listen to all complaints about those who advertise in their pages and will crack down on them. The magazines are to be complimented for making sure you are not cheated. They'll go so far as to permanently refuse future ads from dealers who treat customers unfairly.

The one drawback to mail order is that advertisers can be slow at mailing you the merchandise following receipt of your check. That's because, with the exception of big companies such as Howard's in Ohio, the advertisers are small stores doing mail order on the side or full-time workers who work in the card business in their spare time to pick up extra money. Expect three weeks or more to get your items.

THE CARD SHOW: THE SUPREME OUTLET

Baseball card shows are a recent phenomenon. There were fewer than 50 a year prior to 1984. There were just 10 or 15 a week as late as 1986. Now, with the baseball card and collectibles market booming, there are 60 to 70 shows a week and almost 4,000 a year across the United States. Like cards, they come in all shapes and sizes. The big megashows are held in convention centers or large hotel ballrooms. These usually feature 100 or more dealers with tables or booths and two to eight major stars signing autographs. They pull in 1,000 to 4,000 people a day. Medium-sized shows feature about 75 dealers and one or two stars. They pull in about 700 people a day. Small shows are held in local Holiday Inns, Elks Clubs, Knights of Columbus halls, and high school gyms. They usually have 20 to 40 dealers and maybe a former player who lives in the area on hand to sign autographs. Also, as any community newspaper will tell you, there are even smaller shows held in grade school cafeterias and parks.

No matter what kind of show you go to, you'll find something you need, something you want, and many things you didn't even know existed. If you go to enough shows, you'll find everything—every card imaginable, from the Old Judge cards of the 1880s to the Topps Big Cards of 1989. And there is memorabilia of every kind. A big show is like a traveling Cooperstown. Overall prices are not as low as they are reported to be—there was even blatant overpricing at last year's National Convention—but the large show is your best bet for bargains and good investments.

But you must know how to work a show. There is a big difference between going to a show and "working" a show. A collector who works a show knows how to make the show work for him, not the other way around. You can save a lot of money and make a lot of money if you know what you are doing.

Here's how to work a show for profit, a good collection, and, of course, fun:

1. Set aside the entire afternoon, from three to six hours, for the show. Nobody makes money, gets bargains, or makes a treasure hunt find by running in and out of a show in an hour or less. Some collectors even bracket their time and work a show with a map, sectioning off different areas to hit during different time periods.

2. Bring as much money as you can for bulk purchases. The big savings are in bulk. A $20 card set is quickly dropped to $18 when five sets are purchased. It doesn't sound like much, but if you buy ten sets, you're actually getting a set free. Groupings of cards bring bargains, too. Dealers are looking to make money, lots of it, not recover a particular percent profit on a particular card. A dealer may go down from $20 to $18 on one card, but if you are spending $100 or more with him, he can group ten or eleven cards together and discount.

Most dealers will discount 10 to 15 percent on sales over $25.

Remember that just as you are saving money by buying in bulk, the dealer is saving time by selling in bulk. He is unloading hundreds of dollars worth of merchandise fast, using that money to buy more merchandise.

3. Come late, not early. Most people think all wrong on this. They think that arriving when the show opens, usually at ten A.M., they'll get the best deals and find the best cards—first come, first served. Actually, it's in the early hours that the dealers will not offer discounts. Business is strong then, the lines to get in are long, the stars are signing, the collectors are ready to buy. Why knock off 10 percent in this hot market?

The time to arrive for a show that closes at four P.M. is about one. Spend an hour or two becoming familiar with the merchandise and prices. If dealers have not made a lot of money by three P.M. or so, they'll be willing to drop prices to make a sale. If they have a large inventory on hand that they thought they would sell and don't want to lug home, they'll make deals. Walk up to a guy at 3:55 P.M. during a show that closes at four and offer $100 for eight boxes of '88 Donruss cards that he is selling at $15 a box. Chances are he'll say, Sold! He's unloading things he doesn't want and still takes in $100. At $12.50 a box, he was still making a decent profit (he paid $9 a box). You saved $20.

Valuable cards can be bought at the last minute, too, particularly in bulk. New cards are chancy to begin with, so if you come up at the last minute and offer a dealer ten dollars for ten cards in a plastic case that he's selling at $1.25 each, you may walk away with them.

Even if all the dealers have made a lot of money and have not had to discount much, and even if the crowd has been huge all day, there is something about a last-minute sale and deal that absolutely intrigues the card vendors. At the next show, he'll turn to another dealer and just love to tell the story of how, just as he was packing up, he made a sale.

4. Walk around and look around. One collector spotted a T206 Walter Johnson in Near Mint condition, a $300 card, sitting in a bin of '50s Topps cards. The dealer, eager to unload this oddball card, sold it to him for just $25. Another dealer, who had a pile of old tobacco cards sitting on his table for hours, sold the whole group, worth $200, for less than $100. He had been trying to sell them for six months and was eager.

A boy with $25 in his hand shopped a show, walking around for two hours, until he found a pile of old tobacco and Bowman cards, with a Joe McGinnity stuck in the middle. He knew the McGinnity card was worth $50 and saw that the whole stack was going for $35. He offered his $25 and got them. He then took the cards to another dealer, who specialized in tobacco cards, showed him the McGinnity card, and sold the group for $72. He bought $90 worth of new sets—bulk—for the $72 and in two hours, turned his $25 into $90.

5. Trade at shows. Remember, the new cards in your hand cost you 3¢. Never forget that. One may be worth $4, but it cost you 3¢. Bring lots of new cards (particularly doubles)— stars you can barter with—and trade them for valuable old cards, which are usually a better investment. Try to do full trades—your $50 worth of '85 Clemenses for his one $50 Sandy Koufax. Even if you trade at the 50-60 percent dealer rate, you're getting $2 from him on every $4 card *and the card cost you 3¢*.

Even when making a transaction with a dealer, go for 100 percent trade value. You'll often get it. Offer a dealer $40 worth of your cards for $40 worth of his cards. Don't be intimidated. Remember, his $40 in cards probably cost him only $20, so when he trades with you, he's actually trading $20 for your $40 and is ahead $20. If you have something he wants, he's foolish not to do the deal. And for you, trading even up is better than selling your $40 worth of cards to him for $20.

6. Go shopping. If you have something good to offer, someone at the show has to want what you have. Go to several dealers and listen to offers. The hobby is full of collectors who venture from table to table and, after countless rejections, either get the desired money from a dealer or a fellow collector who overheard him talking to a dealer.

7. Don't waste time at tables where there are no price labels on cards or memorabilia. These dealers aren't interested in bargaining; they are hoping you will offer more than book prices. Also, don't waste time at tables where all cards are overpriced. If you memorize the prices of several popular cards from each set, you can use the prices the dealer is charging for those particular cards to gauge whether he is giving bargains or bad deals on his entire inventory. If you have a lousy memory, just carry around a price guide. If only one card is offered at a bargain rate, check to see if it has been trimmed for better centering. Also: stay away from teenage and college-student dealers—these are hustlers.

8. You will see many dealers with the same display cards. Say you see one dealer selling a '58 Maris for $250 and another dealer on the other side of the room selling the same card in the same condition for $175. If you talk the second dealer down to $150 cash, then you can take your new card and see if the first dealer will buy your card for $200 or give you $200–250 in value in trade. He might not buy your card because he'll insist it isn't in as good condition as you say it is or he'll reveal he has too many '58 Marises as it is (which means he shouldn't be selling one at his rare-card price). But

he may buy it just to keep you from hanging out by his table and offering your Maris to customers for $50 lower than he's charging.

9. Collectors of old cards who aren't interested in mint cards—the best cards for investment—can find low-priced nonmint cards at shows. Almost certainly you'll find some dealer selling commons from the fifties in the $1–2 range. Occasionally you'll find a good bargain, such as a New York player being sold outside the New York area as if he were just a regular common. Also look for dealers' "bargain bins"—boxes with a random selection of loose pre-1970 cards in the $1–2 range. (Be warned that some bargain bins don't contain any bargains.) As shows go on, you'll find more valuable cards in these boxes. Often dealers will be too lazy to return a card to an album after a collector took it out and decided not to buy it. They'll just toss that card into the box. These boxes are useful for filling out sets.

10. If you do much traveling and are able to attend card shows elsewhere, buy cards and memorabilia of players who are more popular in other areas of the country. You'll be able to get good deals on them when you take them to shows in other regions.

11. We have heard collectors run over to dealers, pick up a card, and announce, "This is the card I need to complete a set—I don't care what it costs!" And we have heard customers tell dealers that his particular piece of memorabilia is what they've been looking for everywhere. If you want a bargain, don't say anything. Act as if you don't care if you buy what he has to offer. Don't act impressed by what he has to sell—act amused. Try to talk him down in price even if you're willing to pay what he's charging. If you buy something at a high price, get the dealer's business card in case something isn't right about your purchase and you will want to track him down.

12. Don't worry if you realize after you get home that you should have bought some cards or memorabilia. There will be future shows in which those cards and memorabilia will be offered again. In fact, if you see the same items at the same price at several different shows, inform the dealer that you know they haven't been selling at his price and offer him something lower. You can even try this tack on the second day of a two-day show. After all, if 20,000 other collectors looked at his item and his price and walked on by, it must be overpriced.

GETTING
SERIOUS

CHAPTER 5

BUYING
ON A
BUDGET

Every collector should begin by deciding how much money to spend on cards and collectibles during a specific time period, be it one month, six months, or a full year. Also, know how much you are willing to spend at card shows before you attend them and card shops before you enter them. Set aside a certain amount of money for weekly or monthly candy store card purchases, and don't spend any more than you've planned. And know how much you will offer for an item in an auction, and go no higher if someone matches your bid. Stick to your budget, because this will force you to spend your money prudently. Every collector can make smart deals and clever investments, no matter how little or how much money is available to spend. While there is no perfect, correct strategy to use when buying cards and collectibles to assure the best returns—in our case, we want a fine collection with strong investment potential—there are safe and smart avenues to take, whatever your budget.

A $0–25 BUDGET

Don't worry if you have a small budget. In this hobby you can actually get something for next to nothing—excepting your time and in some cases, postage stamps. If your budget is small, try to get as much free material as possible. Write a baseball team's publicity department and ask for complimentary photos of your favorite players. You will want autographed photos, so write early in the season so the publicists can track down the particular players and secure their autographs. If you receive a photo without an autograph, hang around the ballpark and wait for the player, or if you want a better chance for success, mail the photo directly to the player, with an autograph request. Of course, autograph-seekers needn't only send photos to a player—send Perez-Steele cards, balls, or small pieces of equipment. (Don't forget that you will have to pay return postage.)

Attend promotion days at the ballpark. For the admission price you'll get free shirts, caps, bats, posters, beer mugs, patches, batting gloves, etc. Many items, especially those with a team logo, have immediate value (they were manufactured in limited quantity) and can be sold to fellow collectors and dealers (who wisely always attend giveaway games). Other items might become valuable if you get players to autograph them. When you attend a game, hang on to your ticket stub, buy a program, buy a yearbook, and fight desperately for every foul ball.

Spend $3–5 to go to a card show. Spend between $4 and $12 getting autographs of big-name players. Hall of Famers such as Bob Feller sign autographs for as little as $4—a great collectible, and a great investment. You could conceivably go to one show and get autographs of Feller, Johnny Mize, and future Hall of Famer Rollie Fingers for a total of $12. Or just spend that amount on the autograph of baseball's hottest player, Jose Canseco. But if your budget is small, don't waste it on autographs of fringe players (even ex-Yankees such as Ed Lopat and Joe Collins) unless they're your personal favorites.

At a card show, a bonanza awaits first-time collectors in the magical bargain bins. These are the cardboard boxes or wooden barrels into which a dealer tosses cheap cards that don't move for him. Remember, his interest is in selling Darryl Strawberry rookie cards for $15, so he may take his 1987 and 1988 Darryl Strawberrys, 75¢ to $1 cards, and toss dozens of them into his bargain bin and sell them for a quarter. You can sweep up ten of them, worth $10, for just $2.50. Another great value in bargain bins is the 1983, '84, or '85 common card for a dime. If you know your baseball, you can grab some good players who are on the rise. Orel Hershiser cards, now at $5, were valued at 75¢ two years ago; a bargain-bin digger could have grabbed dozens of Hershisers cheap.

Team sets are another item you should buy immediately. You can get team sets each year—all the players from the '89 Topps set who are Yankees or Tigers, say—for about $2 or $3. This is a great buy. In the Yankee set would be Mattingly; in a Dodger set, Gibson. You not only get a $1–2 card for the $2, but you get the rest of them. The sets usually won't go up in value, but there are exceptions. Suppose you bought a 1987 A's team set for $2; that set included Canseco's individual card as well as McGwire's. Today, the two individuals are at $4 each and the team set is over $10.

If you have $18 to spend, buy the Topps annual set, the soundest investment possible. Fleer, Donruss, and Score sets are also good buys. If you have another $7–10 to spend, supplement the set purchase by acquiring an autograph or two. Or buy several wax and cello packs. In fact, if you have less than the $18 needed for a full set, it would be wise to use your money to buy packs of cards, hoping to find several high-priced cards in the first packs you open. (Are you among the lucky ones who will find Jose Canseco, Mark McGwire, and Don Mattingly in the same pack?) Then you can sell these in-demand cards and have money to buy more cards, perhaps the whole $18 Topps set. If you can afford to wait, hold on to other unopened packs for a year or more—then sell them at a large profit. Unopened packs are among the best investments in the hobby.

Whatever your budget, we recommend that you buy packs of cards—especially if you can stop yourself from opening them all if you find valuable cards in the first packs. (Obviously, if you're trying to put together a set and don't care that much about investments, you should open every pack. But at least get your doubles ready for trades or resale.) If you have money left over after buying packs or have made about $10 in profit, then you might consider buying nonmint cards from the fifties and sixties. Or take a chance and buy in quantity the mint cards of one or two current rookies. After all, if you had guessed that Mike Greenwell had a great future prior to the 1987 season, you could have spent $10 for 100 of his rookie cards and then sold them now for $400. It makes you think.

A $50–75 BUDGET

You've moved up to a higher budget, but start out the same way: buy the annual Topps set for $18. This will leave you with $32 to $57 and several options. One smart move would be to buy a multistar photo for $2, a ball for $4, or a bat for $10 and then attend one or more card shows in order to get several players to sign your items. (Players sometimes charge less for signing photos than balls or bats.) Don't get autographs of random players if you intend for several players to sign the same item; systematically create a valuable theme item by getting the signatures of those specific players who have a special connection: they are Hall of Famers, they play or once played on the same championship team or competed in the World Series, they were MVPs in the same year, they were homer champions, etc. (If you can get all living players who hit over 500 homers to sign the same ball, you've got yourself a great collectible.)

If you aren't interested in autographs, consider the obvious: buy one or two additional card sets, perhaps choosing a Fleer, Donruss, or Score set instead of Topps this time. You will still have money left over to buy packs of cards, but instead of buying loose packs, buy a full unopened box of one of the major sets at a card show for $11 or $12. Since you already have a full set, don't open any of the packs. Keep the box closed and you have a terrific investment, one that will go up dramatically year after year. You may still have a couple of dollars left over. This is about the only time when it wouldn't be a foolish idea to buy a $2–5 boxed set (containing 33 to 44 cards) at the five-and-dime—since these nonmajor-issue sets have little investment potential (although some are quite pleasing to the eye), buy them only after you have bought everything else you want. If the boxed sets still don't interest you, go to a collectibles store, street fair, or garage sale and find some fun, silly, or better, a tremendously underpriced item. (Remember, we told you about a mint Mike Schmidt rookie card that was bought for 25¢ at a recent New Jersey garage sale.)

If you have $57 left over after your initial Topps set purchase, consider spending half of it on a Topps set from a recent year or the entire sum on two Topps sets from recent years. You may also want to consider some of the other major-issue sets. Of course, the only sets you'll be able to buy are those without the expensive rookie card of a superstar player. Indeed, with $57, you may decide that the smart move is to buy one or two of these high-priced rookie cards instead of two full sets, *if* those particular cards have a strong price rate increase year after year. (Check our set charts and do your own homework.) If the player whose rookie card you own does something special and his card prices surge, you will then be able to trade those rookie cards for the two sets you wanted and get something extra besides. (When buying two rookie cards, consider taking two of the same player so that if his card shoots up, you can deal one card and keep the other in your collection.)

A $100–250 BUDGET

With $100–125, you can buy the annual Topps set plus an autographed game-used bat of a top-caliber major leaguer. That's not a bad investment, but you can have a lot more fun with $100. Spread your money around a bit to insure a balanced collection of cards and memorabilia. Unless your budget is $50–150 higher, hold off on buying an expensive autographed bat—instead look for Mike Greenwell or Mark Grace autographed bats for as little as $20—and don't be so quick to buy your Topps set. Instead of buying one set, you now have the resources to buy in bulk. Buy six factory-collated sealed sets for about $100 from dealers at card shows. Keep five sets as investments but open the sixth "free" set and sell or trade the superstar cards, or all the cards of particular teams. Or buy ten boxes in bulk from a dealer for $100 or a little more: sit on them for just two years, and you can make back triple your investment. Or buy two boxes for $22–24—sit on them until they triple in value or immediately rip open the packs in search of high-priced cards to sell or trade. Spend the remainder of your budget on recent full sets; moderately priced recent rookie cards; bats and balls that you will try to get autographed by stars at card shows; the stars' autographs on the balls and bats; and individual cards, including tobacco cards and underpriced cards of superstars of the fifties—if you're not a hard-core investor, look for good deals on nonmint cards.

If you have the money, or a budget close to $250, we recommend that you do all of the above but also buy a case of cards for about $125. Put the case in a closet for four or five years, adding a new case each year. People who stored their 1985 cases could sell them last year for $850–900.

If you don't want to use your extra money to buy a case (perhaps you have no place to store it), buy a more expensive but still moderately priced recent card set, such as the Topps 1985 set or the 1986 Donruss set. Or buy a few more low-priced tobacco cards or superstars of the fifties. Of course, you may want to use over $100 of your $250 to buy one particularly desirable, hot card from the fifties or sixties. With this budget, you can afford it. You can also consider participating in mail, phone, and live auctions in which exotic memorabilia is offered. Just remember that having the money to buy things doesn't mean you should make foolish bids. If you have no luck at auctions, go to antique and collectibles stores in search of memorabilia. With this much money to spend, you can make your collection visually striking, so try to find items to hang on your wall or display in a showcase: pennants, autographed posters, interesting photos, bats, balls, unusual ads featuring baseball legends, etc. Again, don't make any rash purchases—follow our instructions for smart antique shopping.

A $250–500 BUDGET

At this price level, you should definitely buy a case of cards, for about $125. Store it away and wait for it to go up in value. With the rest of your money, diversify. It might be a good idea to spend $100 on different unopened wax boxes. Two years from now, they will be worth at least $150. You may want to spend another $50 buying wax packs in bulk at $10 a box. Of course, if you keep the boxes closed, they will have great investment potential. But even if you keep only one unopened box for future resale, you will do okay. Open four boxes of Topps and you will likely be able to put together two full sets and have doubles of many valuable cards for immediate resale or trade. In four boxes of Fleers, you should get four each of Gregg Jefferies, Jose Canseco, Darryl Strawberry, Wade Boggs, and Kirk Gibson. That's nearly $30 worth of cards right there—and you still have another 2,000 cards!

As in the $100–250 budget, buy six sets of collated factory-sealed sets for about $100. They have great investment potential. As we mentioned, since you are buying in bulk and are actually getting one of these sets for free, you may want to open the extra set and sell or trade its star cards or all the cards for particular teams.

As your budget gets closer to $500, think in terms of older cards and exotic memorabilia. You can now buy a couple of hot $100+ cards from the fifties, or several nonmint cards from that decade. You can buy rare programs, ticket stubs, yearbooks, and press pins—all good investments. You can also buy autographed game-used bats, batting gloves, cleats, caps, and balls. We still recommend that you take the inexpensive route and bring your own items to a card show and get them autographed, rather than buying already autographed items from dealers. But in this price range you can consider buying more expensive items signed by dead or aged Hall of Famers. See what is available and buy items of players whose fame will not diminish. Also make sure that some of your purchases are decorative—you want your collection to look impressive. Just because you have a lot of money to spend, don't forget that many of the most decorative items are relatively inexpensive—don't overlook fairly priced framed advertisements, photos, posters, pennants, etc.

A $500–1,000 BUDGET

The strategy for working with this budget isn't all that different from the one we suggested for working with $250–500. You still can't afford the really expensive baseball cards, you still can't afford to buy all the sets from the eighties, you still can't afford the most expensive memorabilia. But naturally, you can buy a few more $100+ cards—which we recommend doing. (Check out our Hot 100 for some suggestions.) And even after you've bought your case of cards, six sets of factory-collated sealed Topps cards, and $100 worth of unopened boxes, you can finally splurge on a $400 or $500 card, or better for a long-term investment, two or more cards from the same set with a combined value of $400 or $500.

There are a number of great, and undervalued, cards in the $100 to $400 range. Ted Williams cards, in the early years, are still undervalued. Willie Mays cards from the fifties are ridiculously undervalued (in the '57 set, Mantle is $500 and Mays, his equal, just $100). Willie will catch up and you'll have him. The Roger Maris rookie card, which sailed from $27 to $225 from 1986 to 1988, is still considered a good investment by the experts. Cards of all the 500-home-run hitters are good and most are undervalued (Harmon Killebrew's rookie card goes at a ridiculous $100). Many 1948 and 1949 Bowman cards, the small ones, are undervalued; classic buys there are Snider, Satchel Paige, Yogi Berra, and Pee Wee Reese. Early cards of Don Drysdale, Sandy Koufax, and Ernie Banks are still undervalued. Early seventies cards of such stars as Reggie Jackson, Willie Mays, and Carl Yastrzemski can be had at $25 or less. Snap up all you can get; these will soar in the nineties. Other good cards are 1971 and 1972 stars, and if you can find it, the 1962 Topps set with the number 1 Roger Maris card. Great cards, great values. You should also buy unopened wax packs or boxes of cards from previous years. They are expensive, but they will have even more value when you decide to sell them in a year or two.

Significantly, you can now afford much more memorabilia of dead players. Consider buying autographed Babe Ruth or Lou Gehrig items, which every serious collector dreams about owning. You can buy a Ruth ball for $800 or an autographed Lou Gehrig picture for $500. Such items are great investments—but once you have them, you'll likely make them the prizes of your collection. Amazingly, such items are available to you. So are exotic items from almost every other superstar from the past: Ty Cobb, Rogers Hornsby, Joe Jackson, Jackie Robinson. You can even treat yourself to some of the decadent items, such as figurines and commemorative plates—if you like that kind of collectible. You can even consider buying some uniforms of nonsuperstars for about $200. One great item you should consider is the fabled Maris–Mantle autographed ball, which would highlight any collection. You can afford it at $300—especially when you consider it has gone up 60 percent in just two years and has by no means leveled off. Contact a dealer. Also keep an eye out for reasonably priced autographed game-used bats from stars such as Mattingly, Mays, Schmidt, and Strawberry. Go to antique and collectibles stores—you can afford rare or one-of-a-kind items.

A $1,000–5,000 BUDGET

Even when you have a large budget, you should not spend money needlessly. Continue to pass on autographed items of living players that are being offered by dealers and other collectors; create your own collectibles by taking photos, Perez-Steele cards, balls, bats, and equipment to card shows and having the players personally autograph them. You will save a lot of money this way and should also end up with a more valuable item than you would get in a direct dealer purchase.

Continue to buy new cards in the same way we suggested for smaller budgets. Buy a case for about $125, six factory-collated sealed sets (five to keep) for about $100, $100 of unopened boxes, loose unopened packs, and if you want to speculate, lots of rookies you think will become stars. Yes, you may want to double up on everything now that you are working with a higher budget.

Definitely make a commitment to buy older cards. Buy unopened packs and boxes, even a case. These are great investments, which you will sell off at high profits—or open when you know that whatever is inside will be worth much more than it is today. Buy card sets from the eighties before they shoot up in price. Pay attention to what is happening in the current season to see if any veteran player might set a record that by the end of the season will dramatically increase the price of his rookie card *and* the set that includes it. For instance, you would have made a lot of money if you bought up Donruss 1986 sets early in the 1988 season when it first became apparent that Jose Canseco (whose first card is in that set) was on track to become the first player to hit 40 homers and steal 40 bases in one season. If the players who made the Topps 1985 set so expensive start out slowly in the 1989 season, you may reason that the set will drop in value soon after—so make your purchases accordingly.

With $5,000 you may even consider buying a full set from the fifties. You can afford a $3,500 set, but still try to barter—the dealer will lower his price. A fifties set is an exciting purchase and a good investment since they are becoming increasingly difficult to find, particularly in mint condition. We think it may be equally smart to buy sixties sets at lower prices—when we hit the nineties, these sets will jump in value and probably have a higher yearly price rate increase than the fifties sets. Also, consider buying seventies sets; you can buy a 1973 set, one of the nicest, for about $525.

With $5,000 you might gamble on prestigious $1,000 cards. Their book price will go up, but understand that not many collectors will buy such cards from you without a large discount. You may get stuck with them or have to sell them for less than $1,000. That's why it's probably wiser to buy several lower-priced cards from the same set that equal $1,000 in total value—this is a much stronger investment, anyway. Hunt for cards that go for $100 to $500. Buy the rookie cards of Tom Seaver, Ernie Banks, Hank Aaron, Al Kaline, Johnny Bench, Carl Yastrzemski, etc. Perhaps buy two of everything, wait a year, then sell off your doubles.

You must get Ruth and Gehrig autographed material. Get as much material of Hall of Famers as you can. Also buy material of future Hall of Famers. Buy material of hot players such as Jose Canseco, Wade Boggs, Orel Hershiser, Gregg Jefferies, Darryl Strawberry, and Rookie of the Year candidates. (Check our Hot 100 list.) Buy material that illustrates the history of baseball: Negro League items; gloves, game-used bats, uniforms, and equipment of famous players; player contracts; ticket stubs and programs to important games; yearbooks of championship, first-season, or defunct teams; advertising posters; lithographs; personal letters signed by players, managers, and owners; even stadium chairs; etc.

A BUDGET OF $5,000–10,000

With this high budget, you can get tremendous deals on wax and cello packs, sets, boxes, and cases if you buy in bulk. We definitely advise that you do make some bulk purchases. You particularly want to buy full sets. Also buy high-priced pre-1970 cards, dabbling in tobacco, Goudey, Play Ball, and Leaf cards as well as Bowman and Topps. Load up on medium-priced cards of superstars from the fifties, especially those that have shown consistent price increases in the last few years. (See our set charts.)

Consider buying one of the treasured $1,000 cards—including a Mickey Mantle card!—or several cards from the same set that total $1,000 in value. Buy rookie cards of players such as Steve Carlton, Reggie Jackson, and Tom Seaver. These guys are can't-miss, money-in-the-bank future Hall of Famers. Their cards go for $100 to $500. (If you have a smaller budget, you can get them cheaper in excellent condition.) You can buy three of them from one dealer and he'll knock off 15 percent for bulk purchases. These cards should double in value in five years.

Concentrate on memorabilia of dead Hall of Famers. Buy autographed items of Babe Ruth, Lou Gehrig, Ty Cobb, Walter Johnson, etc. See if you can find a ball, bat, or photo on which there are numerous autographs of baseball legends. Buy game-used bats of current Hall of Famers and players who will eventually be inducted. Also consider buying uniforms of star players, which go for $800 to $5,000. Search for autographed gloves and unusual photos with several star players. Buy programs and yearbooks. Buy impressive one-of-a-kind collectibles, items you can hang on your wall or place prominently in your showcase. For such items, go to card shows and auctions and contact sports collectibles shops. Be sure to bargain the prices down, even if you can afford the initial prices. Remember, no matter how high your budget is, you want to get the best deals possible.

CHAPTER 6

THE HOT
100

These are the 100 "movers" in the card market. They are the most heavily traded, the blue chippers, the hits with a bullet, the top of the charts, the Good Housekeeping seal of approval. But some of them shouldn't be; they've gone as high as they're going to. Some are packs, some are sets, some are individual cards. Collectively, they are the 100 most traded, bought, sold, and talked-about cards. They are what everyone tells you to buy. They may be wrong. Listen.

(Bow-Bowman, CJ-Cracker Jacks, Don-Donruss, F-Fleer, T-Topps, Topps Tr-Topps Traded)

PLAYER/SET/ETC.	1985	1986	1987	1988	1989*	PRICE RATE INC.**
1. Jose Canseco ('86Don)	—	$.25	$2	$7	$75	300x
Canseco ('87T)	—	—	$.25	$3	$7	28x
2. Wade Boggs ('83T)	$3.75	$5.25	$12	$30	$34	9.1x
3. Darryl Strawberry ('84F)	$1.50	$2.50	$7.50	$10	$15	10x
4. Roger Maris ('58T)	$20	$27	$50	$225	$275	13.8x
5. Joe Jackson ('14CJ)	$200	$350	$600	$1,200	$2,500	12.5x
6. Ernie Banks ('54T)	$55	$65	$100	$300	$550	10x
7. Duke Snider ('52T)	$32	$45	$90	$200	$250	8x
8. Babe Ruth #181 ('33 Goudey)	$375	$600	$900	$3,000	$3,600	9.6x
9. Bob Uecker ('62T)	$6	$13	$35	$90	$90	15x
10. George Bell ('82F)	$.35	$.80	$1.50	$7	$6	17.1x
11. Mickey Mantle ('51 Bow)	$400	$500	$800	$4,700	$4,700	11.8x
12. '85T wax pack	$.40	$1.50	$2.50	$3.50	$4	10x
13. '85 Donruss box	$14	$40	$85	$100	$110	7.9x
14. Mark McGwire ('85T)	$.25	$.25	$.50	$17	$15	60x
15. '85 Topps set	$17	$22	$55	$90	$100	5.9x
16. Eric Davis ('85T)	$.35	$2	$1	$10	$11	31x
17. Roger Clemens ('85T)	$.40	$.80	$8	$10	$10	25x

*Projected.
**From 1985 to 1989.

THE HOT 100

PLAYER/SET/ETC.	1985	1986	1987	1988	1989*	PRICE RATE INC.**
18. Kirby Puckett ('85T)	$.50	$1	$6	$8	$10	20x
19. Don Mattingly ('84T)	$4.45	$5.50	$35	$27	$27	6.1x
20. Don Mattingly ('85T)	$.40	$1.20	$8	$10	$10	25x
21. Dwight Gooden ('85T)	$3	$6	$7	$8	$11	3.7x
22. '33 Goudey Set	$4,500	$6,200	$9,000	$18,000	$24,000	5.3x
23. Tris Speaker ('33 Goudey)	$40	$70	$100	$140	$180	4.5x
24. Lou Gehrig ('33 Goudey)	$200	$325	$500	$1,700	$2,500	12.5x
25. Dizzy Dean ('33 Goudey)	$100	$180	$250	$350	$400	4x
26. T206 set (without Wagner, Plank, Magie)	$6,600	$9,000	$17,000	$27,000	$36,000	5.5x
27. Topps '61 set	$730	$935	$1,400	$3,600	$3,800	5.2x
28. Topps '62 set	$470	$650	$950	$3,200	$3,400	7.2x
29. Topps '60 set	$430	$550	$800	$2,500	$3,000	7x
30. Topps '59 set	$440	$575	$850	$2,800	$3,100	7x
31. Topps '58 set	$470	$650	$1,000	$2,800	$3,300	7x
32. Topps '57 set	$770	$1,050	$1,600	$4,500	$4,800	6.2x
33. Topps '56 set	$640	$850	$1,250	$3,600	$4,200	6.6x
34. Topps '55 set	$600	$850	$1,250	$3,500	$4,200	7x
35. Topps '54 set	$820	$1,100	$1,500	$4,800	$5,800	7.1x
36. Topps '53 set	$1,800	$2,200	$3,000	$8,000	$9,000	5x
37. Topps '52 set	$9,600	$15,000	$18,000	$36,000	$38,000	4x
38. Bowman '53 set (color)	$1,800	$2,250	$2,750	$6,000	$7,200	4x

PLAYER/SET/ETC.	1985	1986	1987	1988	1989*	PRICE RATE INC.**
39. Bowman '55 set	$550	$725	$1,000	$3,300	$3,600	6.5x
40. Eddie Mathews ('60 Post cereal)	$130	$150	$175	$200	$240	1.8x
41. Willie Mays ('51 Bow)	$340	$400	$600	$1,100	$1,300	3.8x
42. Ty Cobb (T206) (portrait/green)	$250	$425	$800	$1,000	$1,200	4.8x
43. Christy Mathewson (T206)	$60	$120	$200	$250	$300	5x
44. Walter Johnson (T206)	$65	$125	$250	$300	$350	5.4x
45. Ted Williams ('40 Play Ball)	$150	$225	$300	$650	$950	6.3x
46. Hank Aaron ('54T)	$175	$225	$325	$500	$700	4x
47. Yogi Berra ('52T)	$40	$55	$90	$200	$250	6.2x
48. Andy Pafko ('52T)	$125	$225	$350	$550	$1,200	9.6x
49. Roy Campanella ('52T)	$350	$450	$650	$775	$1,100	3.1x
50. '56 Dodger Team (T)	$12	$18	$24	$65	$85	7x
51. 1971 Topps set	$385	$500	$650	$1,000	$1,200	3.1x
52. Sandy Koufax ('55T)	$60	$80	$125	$250	$400	6.7x
53. Pete Rose ('63T)	$300	$450	$500	$550	$550	1.8x
54. Mickey Mantle ('52T)	$2,100	$2,900	$3,300	$6,500	$6,500	3.1x
55. Frank "Home Run" Baker (T206)	$25	$35	$60	$100	$125	5x
56. Pee Wee Reese ('52T)	$225	$275	$350	$450	$550	2.4x
57. Mike Schmidt ('73T)	$65	$70	$125	$150	$200	3x

THE HOT 100

PLAYER/SET/ETC.	1985	1986	1987	1988	1989*	PRICE RATE INC.**
58. Satchel Paige ('53T)	$40	$60	$90	$200	$220	5.5x
59. Reggie Jackson ('69T)	$60	$70	$100	$200	$220	3.7x
60. Joe Tinker (T206)	$20	$35	$80	$100	$120	6x
61. Johnny Evers (T206)	$25	$40	$80	$100	$120	4.8x
62. Cy Young (T206)	$42	$70	$125	$150	$200	4.8x
63. Honus Wagner (T206)	$25,000	$32,000	$36,000	$36,000	$36,000	1.4x
64. Fred Merkle (T206)	$10	$14	$25	$25	$30	3x
65. '49 Bowman commons	$16	$20	$27	$45	$55	3.4x
66. '64 Aaron (Bazooka)	$24	$30	$35	$45	$55	2.3x
67. '52 Early Wynn (Red Man)	$7	$7.50	$10	$15	$20	2.8x
68. Cal Ripken ('82T)	$5.50	$6.25	$9	$12	$14	2.5x
69. Tony Gwynn ('83T)	$3.25	$3.50	$8	$16	$18	5.6x
70. Andre Dawson ('77T)	$9	$8	$6	$25	$42	4.7x
71. Dave Winfield ('74T)	$14	$18	$18	$25	$40	2.8x
72. Alan Trammell ('78T)	$7	$11	$9	$28	$35	5x
73. Gary Carter ('75T)	$11	$14	$35	$40	$50	4.5x
74. Jim Rice ('75T)	$18	$18	$35	$40	$30	1.7x
75. Fred Lynn ('75T)	$9	$9	$10	$10	$10	1.1x
76. Keith Hernandez ('75T)	$9	$10	$20	$25	$25	2.9x
77. Fernando Valenzuela ('81T)	$2.50	$4	$7.50	$7.50	$7	2.8x

PLAYER/SET/ETC.	1985	1986	1987	1988	1989*	PRICE RATE INC.**
78. Rickey Henderson ('80T)	$6.50	$12	$22	$28	$32	5x
79. Steve Carlton ('65T)	$100	$105	$110	$100	$120	1.2x
80. Harmon Killebrew ('55T)	$26	$34	$60	$100	$220	8.5x
81. Nolan Ryan ('68T)	$35	$50	$80	$125	$150	4.3x
82. Tom Seaver ('67T)	$95	$135	$250	$400	$500	5.3x
83. Billy Martin ('52T)	$30	$40	$75	$150	$200	6.7x
84. Frank Robinson ('57T)	$34	$36	$45	$100	$125	3.7x
85. Bob Feller ('52T)	$20	$30	$50	$90	$100	5x
86. Jocko Conlan ('55 Bow)	$8	$12	$18	$35	$45	5.7x
87. Early Wynn ('55 Bow)	$6	$7	$7.50	$17	$19	3.2x
88. Sal Maglie ('55 Bow)	$1.50	$1.50	$2	$4	$6	4x
89. Luke Appling ('34 Goudey)	$21	$27	$40	$60	$70	3.3x
90. Charlie Gehringer ('33 Goudey)	$30	$50	$65	$100	$120	4x
91. Mark Grace ('88 Don)	—	—	—	$2	$3	1.5x
92. Mike Greenwell ('87T)	—	—	$.40	$4	$6	15x
93. David Cone ('87 Don)	—	—	$.30	$2	$3	10x
94. Gregg Jefferies ('88 Don)	—	—	—	$3	$8	2.7x
95. Johnny Bench ('68T)	$100	$110	$120	$125	$190	1.9x
96. Carl Yastrzemski ('60T)	$80	$120	$140	$150	$200	2.5x
97. 1988 Topps Traded set	—	—	—	$9	$12	1.3x

PLAYER/SET/ETC.	1985	1986	1987	1988	1989*	PRICE RATE INC.**
98. 1986 Donruss set	—	$18	$40	$85	$110	6.1x
99. Chris Sabo ('88 Topps Tr)	—	—	—	$1.50	$2.50	1.7x
100. Andres Galarraga ('86 Don)	—	$.20	$.80	$5	$6	30x

BEST ROOKIE BETS FOR 1989: Sandy Alomar, Jr., Ken Griffey, Jr., Ricky Jordan, Gary Sheffield, and Gregg Jefferies (Topps).

BEST FUTURE STARS: '88 Olympians Jim Abbott, Robin Ventura, Ty Griffin, Andy Benes, and Maurice Vaughan.

HOT 100 NOTES

All cards are compared from 1985 to the present because 1985 was the first real year of the card explosion. To say a card went up 145 times from 1973 to 1989 is meaningless because it may not have increased at all since 1985. However, if it climbed 40x from 1985 to 1989 it's meaningful.

In 1987, *Sports Collectors Digest* and *Beckett's Monthly,* the leading price-guide publications, doubled their old card prices within six months—hence the big leap that year.

Below are notes to guide you on buying, and not buying, cards or sets on the "Hot 100." Items to avoid are in italics.

1. Canseco—an MVP in '88, young, strong, clean-living, big, good eye, plays with McGwire on a championship contender. He's got everything going, just everything—the Mantle of

the era. Still, $75 for the '86 card is nuts; buy the Topps '87 at $7 instead.

2. Boggs—consistent .350 hitter (hit .350 even during sex scandal last year) and sure Hall of Famer. The best card in America for investment.

3. Strawberry—power hitter, from New York, and still a big future.

4. Maris—tied to Mantle, a Yankee and possible Hall of Famer. The last year saw big surge in Maris and 1989 should, too.

5. Jackson—The film *Eight Men Out* should eventually push Shoeless Joe up over the $3,000 mark and he'll climb—great and notorious.

7. Snider—Dodger, autograph superstar, and home run hitter.

8. Ruth—will always be good investment.

9. *Uecker—silliness in Ueck cards will die fast. Don't buy!*

10. *Bell—falling fast. Avoid.*

11. *Mantle—the peak has been reached. Don't buy.*

12. '85T—at less than $3, buy. More than $3, no.

14. McGwire—price went up, then down, but should climb back.

15. '85 Topps Set—should keep rising.

17. *Clemens—pitchers don't climb. Avoid at $10 or over.*

18. Puckett—a potential giant, even from Minnesota. Buy.

19–20. *Mattingly '85s and '84s—too many on market, will stall. Don't buy unless you're a Yankee lover.*

21. Gooden—Dr. K is okay. Will climb slowly but surely.

22. 1933 Goudey Set—went from $4,500 to $24,000 in four years. How much did your house go up?

23. Speaker—old, Goudey, a great. Buy.

24. Gehrig—even his VG cards have gone from $40 to $300. Buy. A can't miss and a rare card.

26. T206 Set—*Eight Men Out* should fuel old-timer interest. If you have money, a good bet, even at $36,000. Undiscovered area.

27–37. Topps Sets From 1952 to 1961—they've gone up four to seven times—steady climbs over the years. Sets are your very best investment, regardless of price.

39. Bowman '55 Set—the TV cards and center of big revival.

40. *Eddie Mathews—the guides keep the price high, but this one hasn't moved and won't. Forget him.*

41. Mays '51 Bowman—Willie may never reach Mickey's prices, but there's still a lot of room for him to go up from here.

42. Cobb T206—the coming boom in tobacco cards will send prices on Cobb skyrocketing.

43–44. *Mathewson and Johnson—see #40 above.*

45. Ted Williams Playball 1940—Williams still undervalued. Will climb.

46. Aaron '54T—still unappreciated, but will be. Good bet.

47. Yogi Berra—everybody loves Yogi. A great investment.

48. *Pafko—high only because it's the No. 1 card in '52 set. Try to find a dealer who will tell you the card is mint. They really chisel on this one. Avoid like the plague.*

49. Campanella—beloved and a Dodger. Can't-miss investment.

50. Dodger Team—again, the Dodgers. They have their own army. Good bet for years to come.

53. *Rose—this card climbed when Pete broke hit record, but has leveled off at $500 or so. He'll go in Hall, but his cards are way overvalued. It won't climb that much. Besides, market is flooded with Rose rookie counterfeits.*

54. *Mantle—the Mick's cards have leveled off. Poor investment.*

55. Baker—the tobacco cards are the next big boom—buy, buy, buy.

57. Schmidt—a sure Hall of Famer and potential 600 HR hitter. He'll leap. Buy.

58. Paige—the legend will grow. Buy.

59. Jackson—another sure shot Hall of Famer. Good investment.

63. *Honus Wagner—at $36,000 (and stalled there) a poor investment. Why not do something crazy with the $36,000—like put your child through college?*

65. *Bowman commons—avoid. You'll never resell commons.*

66. *Aaron—the bubble-gum bubble burst on the Bazooka sets long ago.*

67. *Wynn—The Red Man set has the prettiest cards ever made, but the prices have pretty much stalled. A pity.*

68. *Ripken—he's a great hitter, a great fielder, a fine fellow— but he plays in Baltimore on a terrible team. Avoid.*

69. Gwynn—he's never caught on as investment. But he has a shot at the Hall.

70. *Dawson—his career peaked in '87.*

71. Winfield—super '88 season and a Yankee. Still good investment, even at high prices.

72. *Trammell—overrated and overpriced—unless there will be a push to make him Hall candidate, on Robin Yount level.*

73. Carter—at tail end of career. Card will stall. However, a good hedge since he's probably a Hall of Famer 8–9 years from now.

74. *Jim Rice—a dud.*

76. Hernandez—New York, an All-Star, and top hitter, but his card is leveling off.

77. *Valenzuela—his market is crashing.*

78. Henderson—the top investment, surpassed only by Boggs. He's a good hitter, had a good '88 season, and plays in New York. In 2–3 years Rickey will break Lou Brock's all-time base-stealing record and then his card will soar, like the '85 Rose boom. Buy.

79. Carlton—A sure Hall of Famer; even though his card's stalled, it's certain to go up over the next five years.

81. Ryan—underrated card, a prospective Hall of Famer and will go up.

82. Seaver—even at $500, a good investment. He's New York, a 300-game winner, and a certain Hall of Famer. PLUS—that all-American-boy charm. A big, big card in the future.

83. Martin—the collectors love Billy.

84. Robinson—never appreciated.

85. Feller—a steady climber because his many personal appearances keep him in the public eye.

86. *Conlan—umpires? No.*

88. Maglie—never a strong card outside of New York, but strong in New York because he pitched for the Dodgers, Giants, and Yankees.

89. *Appling—the Michael Dukakis of cards: people like him, but they don't buy him.*

90. *Gehringer—see Appling.*

91. Grace—a strong card for the future.

92. Greenwell—the next Yaz. Buy.

93. Cone—buy, but remember that all pitchers peak at around $12.

94. Jefferies—the mystery of the pyramids. Will he be too high at $8 after one month in the majors? Or is he too low for the greatness predicted? The jury is still out.

95. Bench—the recent Hall of Famer's prices will climb this spring.

96. Yastrzemski—this recent Hall of Famer's prices will go up 40–50 percent this year.

97. 1988 Topps Traded set—will explode in 1990, when all the Olympians in it are in the bigs. Buying this now, even at $12, is like buying stock in the Wright Brothers while they were still into bicycles.

98. *1986 Donruss set—the single biggest mistake of the century would be to buy this. When Canseco mania subsides, the set will stall. Avoid.*

99. *Sabo—better to buy the whole set than speculate on his card.*

100. *Galarraga—good player. No national image. Avoid.*

CHAPTER 7

SET CHARTS

What follows are charts for all popular card sets from 1909 to 1985, the year prices for most cards exploded. We have tracked prices for both the sets and the highest-priced cards in those sets from 1980 to 1988, with special attention to the pivotal period 1985–88. We have also projected prices for 1989: consult a monthly price guide to see if sets and cards reached, surpassed, or stopped short of expectations. Prices are for mint-condition and near-mint cards.

Look over these charts to determine which full sets might fit your investment needs. Simply see which sets have had strong price and price rate increases, especially between 1985 and 1988; are projected to increase further by 1989; and (look at your latest price guide) are doing as well as we projected. The charts give the prices of particular sets, as well as the number of high-priced cards and low-priced commons that are contained in the set, should you want to try to put a set together yourself. (No, no one can afford to do this with the Topps 1952 set.) But the best way to use the charts is to help you decide which individual cards to acquire and which to leave alone. The smaller investor should concentrate on the far-less-expensive post-1970s sets, but don't overlook the affordable bargains to be found in the older sets.

The following is our best advice about how to choose cards for investment:

1. Find cards that have had price rate increases since 1985 higher or comparable to that of the set that contains them. Steady price rate increases have made sets the best investments in the hobby; cards that outperform the sets are worth grabbing *fast*.

2. Find high-priced cards that have had large, steady price increases since 1985. This includes some cards that have *not* had impressive price rate increases. Remember that it is essential for a card to have a large price jump if you want to sell it back to the dealer you bought it from for even a little above what you paid.

3. If you're looking for a low-priced bargain, try this: Find star players whose cards are included in several of our set charts, signifying that they are among those sets' highest-priced cards. Then find those sets that don't include cards of those players. You'll notice, for instance, that even the likes of Hank Aaron, Willie Mays, and Sandy Koufax are, for no good reason, missing in certain years. Once the listed high-priced cards in these sets peak and stall, those star players' cards will—because the nation's dealers will see to it—become hot and move up in value. Buy them now, while they're still cheap.

4. Find star players on our charts (and in your price guides) who had their rookie cards in the same year. If the rookie cards are comparably priced and their careers were similar, it stands to reason that all subsequent cards should be comparably priced year after year. If they aren't, snap up the lower-priced card; it should eventually rise to the level of the other one. (An example: the rookie cards of Ernie Banks and Al Kaline were both issued in 1954. Both cards were priced at $300 in 1988 and are projected to jump to $550 in 1989. Year after year, their cards are similarly priced, which makes sense since they had comparable Hall of Fame careers. However, for no known reason, the Banks 1955 Bowman is priced at $200, while the Kaline 1955 Bowman sells for $50. Buy Kaline now, before anyone else realizes that his card should be priced at Banks's level.)

5. For pre-1970 sets, instead of buying one high-priced card, buy several lower-priced cards (including duplicates) from the same set whose total value equals that of the higher-priced card. In other words, choose three $200 cards instead of one $600 card. (Or trade one high-priced card for several cards of equal value.) Almost without exception—Mickey Mantle cards being the exception—the price increase of a single card between 1985 and 1988 was much less than the total increase for several cards over the same period.

T206 1909–11
(513 CARDS/APPROX. 30 COMMONS)

CARDS	1980 PRICE	1985 PRICE	$ INCREASE SINCE 1985	RATE INCREASE SINCE 1985	1988 PRICE	1989 PROJECTED PRICE
SET (without Big Four)*	$2,500	$6,600	$20,400	4.09x	$27,000	$36,000
Wagner**	$8,000	$25,000	$11,000	1.4x	$36,000	$36,000
JDoyle*** (NY Nat'l)			$10,000	10,000x+	$10,000	$10,000
Plank	$3,500	$6,000	$2,000	1.3x	$8,000	$10,000
Magie (error)	$500	$2,200	$3,300	2.5x	$5,500	$6,500
Demitt (St. Louis)	$150	$600	$1,200	3x	$1,800	$2,100
O'Hara	$150	$400	$1,000	3.5x	$1,400	$1,800
Cobb (portrait/ green)	$60	$250	$750	4x	$1,000	$1,200
Cobb (bat on shoulder)	$50	$200	$700	4.5x	$900	$1,150
Cobb (bat off shoulder)	$50	$200	$600	4x	$800	$1,100
Cobb (portrait/red)	$50	$160	$540	4.4x	$700	$950
Elberfeld (portrait/ Washington)	$65	$200	$500	3.5x	$700	$900

*The Big Four are the rare Wagner, Plank, Doyle variation, and "Magie" error cards.
**Although Wagner's card is priced at $36,000 in mint condition, such cards have sold for almost triple that amount.
***The existence of a Joe Doyle variation card marked "N.Y. Nat'l." was not known in 1980 or 1985. Two such cards have since been discovered and are valued at $10,000 each.

SET CHARTS

T205 GOLD BORDER 1911
(280 CARDS/APPROX. 120 COMMONS)

CARDS	1980 PRICE	1985 PRICE	$ INCREASE SINCE 1985	RATE INCREASE SINCE 1985	1988 PRICE	1989 PROJECTED PRICE
SET	$1,050	$3,200	$13,800	5.3x	$17,000	$21,000
Cobb	$60	$250	$650	3.6x	$900	$1,200
Hoblitzel (no stats)	$4	$12	$288	25x	$300	$400
WJohnson	$25	$80	$220	3.75x	$300	$350
Mathewson	$20	$60	$240	5x	$300	$400
Speaker	$20	$60	$165	3.75x	$225	$300
Wallace	$30	$60	$165	3.75x	$225	$300
Young	$20	$60	$165	3.75x	$225	$300
ECollins	$30	$60	$140	3.3x	$200	$250

T207 1912
(200 CARDS/APPROX. 120 COMMONS)

CARDS	1980 PRICE	1985 PRICE	$ INCREASE SINCE 1985	RATE INCREASE SINCE 1985	1988 PRICE	1989 PROJECTED PRICE
SET	$4,500	$6,400	$13,600	3.1x	$20,000	$24,000
Lowdermilk	$525	$600	$1,100	2.8x	$1,700	$2,200
ILewis (emblem)	$525	$600	$1,100	2.8x	$1,700	$2,200
ILewis	$525	$600	$1,100	2.8x	$1,700	$2,200

continued

CARDS	1980 PRICE	1985 PRICE	$ INCREASE SINCE 1985	RATE INCREASE SINCE 1985	1988 PRICE	1989 PROJECTED PRICE
WMiller	$250	$600	$1,100	2.8x	$1,700	$2,200
Speaker	$70	$125	$325	3.6x	$450	$550
Saier	$125	$180	$220	2.2x	$400	$400
GTyler	$125	$180	$220	2.2x	$400	$400

Goudey 1933
(239–40 CARDS/APPROX. 150 COMMONS)

CARDS	1980 PRICE	1985 PRICE	$ INCREASE SINCE 1985	RATE INCREASE SINCE 1985	1988 PRICE	1989 PROJECTED PRICE
SET (without Lajoie)	$6,500	$4,500	$13,500	4x	$18,000	$24,000
Lajoie	$4,500	$6,000	$3,000	1.5x	$9,000	$18,000
Ruth No. 181	$200	$375	$2,625	8x	$3,000	$3,600
Ruth No. 53	$200	$375	$2,425	7.5x	$2,800	$3,300
Ruth No. 149	$200	$375	$2,425	7.5x	$2,800	$3,300
Ruth No. 144	$175	$300	$2,200	8.3x	$2,500	$3,000
Gehrig No. 92	$125	$200	$1,500	8.5x	$1,700	$2,500
Gehrig No. 160	$125	$200	$1,500	8.5x	$1,700	$2,500
Bengough*	$50	$125	$475	4.8x	$600	$800
DDean	$50	$100	$250	3.5x	$350	$400

*Bengough is the first card of the set; first and last cards are usually expensive regardless of the caliber of the player depicted.

DIAMOND STARS 1934–36
(108 CARDS/APPROX. 70 COMMONS)

CARDS	1980 PRICE	1985 PRICE	$ INCREASE SINCE 1985	RATE INCREASE SINCE 1985	1988 PRICE	1989 PROJECTED PRICE
SET	$1,500	$2,200	$3,800	2.7x	$6,000	$7,200
Dickey No. 103	$100	$125	$200	2.6x	$325	$400
Grove '34	$30	$80	$170	3.1x	$250	$350
Grove '35	$30	$80	$170	3.1x	$250	$350
Traynor No. 99	$90	$125	$125	2x	$250	$300
Averill No. 100	$60	$80	$120	2.5x	$200	$250
Lopez No. 97	$60	$80	$80	2x	$160	$170
Lombardi No. 105	$45	$55	$105	2.9x	$160	$170
Berger No. 108	$40	$55	$105	2.9x	$160	$200
Rolfe No. 104	$40	$55	$75	2.4x	$130	$155
Foxx	$25	$50	$60	2.2x	$110	$130

GOUDEY 1934
(96 CARDS/APPROX. 65 COMMONS)

CARDS	1980 PRICE	1985 PRICE	$ INCREASE SINCE 1985	RATE INCREASE SINCE 1985	1988 PRICE	1989 PROJECTED PRICE
SET	$1,500	$2,200	$7,800	4.5x	$10,000	$15,000
Gehrig No. 37	$135	$250	$1,550	7.2x	$1,800	$2,400

continued

GETTING SERIOUS

CARDS	1980 PRICE	1985 PRICE	$ INCREASE SINCE 1985	RATE INCREASE SINCE 1985	1988 PRICE	1989 PROJECTED PRICE
Gehrig No. 61	$135	$250	$1,550	7.2x	$1,800	$2,400
Foxx	$35	$125	$275	3.2x	$400	$525
DDean	$50	$100	$175	2.8x	$275	$300
DeShong*	$40	$65	$160	3.5x	$225	$300

*DeShong is the last card of the set; first and last cards are usually expensive regardless of the caliber of the player depicted.

PLAY BALL 1939
(161 CARDS/APPROX. 130 COMMONS)

CARDS	1980 PRICE	1985 PRICE	$ INCREASE SINCE 1985	RATE INCREASE SINCE 1985	1988 PRICE	1989 PROJECTED PRICE
SET	$1,050	$1,400	$4,100	3.9x	$5,500	$6,800
DiMaggio	$110	$200	$600	4x	$300	$1,200
DiMaggio (error)	$110	$200	$500	3.5x	$700	$1,050
TWilliams (name in upper and lower case)	$90	$150	$525	4.5x	$675	$1,000
TWilliams (name in upper case)	$90	$150	$500	4.3x	$650	$950
Averill	$18	$36	$64	2.8x	$100	$110

SET CHARTS

PLAY BALL 1940
(240 CARDS/APPROX. 160 COMMONS)

CARDS	1980 PRICE	1985 PRICE	$ INCREASE SINCE 1985	RATE INCREASE SINCE 1985	1988 PRICE	1989 PROJECTED PRICE
SET	$1,250	$1,800	$7,700	5.3x	$9,500	$12,000
DiMaggio	$150	$250	$650	3.6x	$900	$1,200
TWilliams	$90	$150	$500	4.3x	$650	$950
SJJackson	$20	$90	$360	5x	$450	$700

PLAY BALL 1941
(72 CARDS/APPROX. 45 COMMONS)

CARDS	1980 PRICE	1985 PRICE	$ INCREASE SINCE 1985	RATE INCREASE SINCE 1985	1988 PRICE	1989 PROJECTED PRICE
SET	$640	$1,300	$3,700	3.8x	$5,000	$6,200
DiMaggio	$250	$325	$525	2.6x	$850	$1,050
TWilliams	$100	$180	$420	3.3x	$600	$850

LEAF 1948—49
(98 CARDS/APPROX. 85 COMMONS)

CARDS	1980 PRICE	1985 PRICE	$ INCREASE SINCE 1985	RATE INCREASE SINCE 1985	1988 PRICE	1989 PROJECTED PRICE
SET	$3,700	$4,000	$9,000	3.25x	$13,000	$16,000
Paige	$325	$360	$440	2.22x	$800	$950
Feller	$250	$250	$300	2.2x	$550	$650
DiMaggio	$125	$150	$350	3.33x	$500	$625
Ruth	$125	$175	$325	2.9x	$500	$600
Kell	$80	$120	$205	2.7x	$325	$400
Slaughter	$120	$120	$205	2.7x	$325	$400
TWilliams	$90	$90	$185	3.1x	$275	$375
JRobinson	$60	$70	$155	3.2x	$225	$325
Doby	$90	$80	$145	2.8x	$225	$300

BOWMAN 1948
(48 CARDS/APPROX. 14 COMMONS)

CARDS	1980 PRICE	1985 PRICE	$ INCREASE SINCE 1985	RATE INCREASE SINCE 1985	1988 PRICE	1989 PROJECTED PRICE
SET	$325	$425	$1,075	3.5x	$1,500	$1,900
Musial	$52	$75	$150	3x	$225	$300
Berra	$20	$44	$131	4x	$175	$250
Rizzuto	$35	$35	$75	3.1x	$110	$150

SET CHARTS

BOWMAN 1949
(240 CARDS/APPROX. 145 COMMONS)

CARDS	1980 PRICE	1985 PRICE	$ INCREASE SINCE 1985	RATE INCREASE SINCE 1985	1988 PRICE	1989 PROJECTED PRICE
SET	$2,500	$2,700	$5,800	3.1x	$8,500	$10,500
Paige	$350	$350	$400	2.1x	$750	$1,000
Snider	$175	$200	$325	2.6x	$525	$725
JRobinson	$50	$65	$210	4.2x	$275	$400
Musial	$50	$65	$135	3.1x	$200	$275
Ashburn	$25	$40	$135	4.4x	$175	$250
Campanella	$32	$50	$125	3.5x	$175	$225
Lemon	$85	$60	$90	2.5x	$150	$200
Berra	$26	$32	$93	3.9x	$125	$175
Rizzuto	$12.50	$30	$70	3.3x	$100	$150

BOWMAN 1950
(252 CARDS/APPROX. 60 COMMONS)

CARDS	1980 PRICE	1985 PRICE	$ INCREASE SINCE 1985	RATE INCREASE SINCE 1985	1988 PRICE	1989 PROJECTED PRICE
SET	$850	$950	$4,250	5.5x	$5,200	$6,400
TWilliams	$50	$65	$255	4.9x	$320	$500
JRobinson	$45	$56	$194	4.5x	$250	$375

continued

177

GETTING SERIOUS

CARDS	1980 PRICE	1985 PRICE	$ INCREASE SINCE 1985	RATE INCREASE SINCE 1985	1988 PRICE	1989 PROJECTED PRICE
Berra	$23	$32	$168	6.3x	$200	$300
Parnell	$6	$25	$125	6x	$150	$200
Campanella	$27	$36	$114	4.2x	$150	$200
Snider	$14	$22	$103	5.7x	$125	$175

BOWMAN 1951
(324 CARDS/APPROX. 185 COMMONS)

CARDS	1980 PRICE	1985 PRICE	$ INCREASE SINCE 1985	RATE INCREASE SINCE 1985	1988 PRICE	1989 PROJECTED PRICE
SET	$1,550	$1,700	$9,300	6.5x	$11,000	$13,500
Mantle	$375	$400	$4,300	11.8x	$4,700	$4,700
Mays	$325	$340	$760	3.2x	$1,100	$1,300
Ford	$40	$75	$525	8x	$600	$950
TWilliams	$50	$60	$215	4.6x	$275	$325
Berra	$25	$32	$143	5.5x	$175	$225
Snider	$13	$22	$78	4.5x	$100	$125
Dickey	$25	$26	$74	3.8x	$100	$120
Campanella	$25	$32	$68	3.1x	$100	$100

TOPPS BLUE BACKS 1951
(52 CARDS/APPROX. 17 COMMONS)

CARDS	1980 PRICE	1985 PRICE	$ INCREASE SINCE 1985	RATE INCREASE SINCE 1985	1988 PRICE	1989 PROJECTED PRICE
SET	$370	$420	$830	3x	$1,250	$1,550
Mize	$16	$18	$32	2.8x	$50	$75
Ashburn	$10	$13	$27	3.1x	$40	$60
Slaughter	$14	$13	$27	3.1x	$40	$55
Doerr	$8	$9	$31	4.4x	$40	$60

TOPPS CONNIE MACK ALL-STARS 1951
(11 CARDS)

CARDS	1980 PRICE	1985 PRICE	$ INCREASE SINCE 1985	RATE INCREASE SINCE 1985	1988 PRICE	1989 PROJECTED PRICE
SET	$2,500	$2,000	$2,000	2x	$4,000	$5,200
Ruth	$600	$450	$650	2.4x	$1,100	$1,500
Gehrig	$450	$450	$300	1.7x	$750	$800
WJohnson	$350	$300	$25	1.1x	$325	$475
Alexander	$250	$200	$100	1.5x	$300	$300
Mathewson	$130	$120	$180	2.5x	$300	$400
Wagner	$160	$150	$150	2x	$300	$400
Cochrane	$160	$120	$105	1.9x	$225	$250

continued

CARDS	1980 PRICE	1985 PRICE	$ INCREASE SINCE 1985	RATE INCREASE SINCE 1985	1988 PRICE	1989 PROJECTED PRICE
Mack	$210	$150	$75	1.5x	$225	$250
ECollins	$110	$90	$60	1.7x	$150	$180
Speaker	$130	$90	$60	1.7x	$150	$180
JCollins	$70	$70	$55	1.8x	$125	$160

The cards in the two Topps All-Stars sets of 1951 were packaged with a thin piece of plain cardboard at the top of each to protect the cards. The prices above are for cards with these tops; card without tops are worth half as much.

TOPPS CURRENT ALL-STARS 1951
(11 CARDS)

CARDS	1980 PRICE	1985 PRICE	$ INCREASE SINCE 1985	RATE INCREASE SINCE 1985	1988 PRICE	1989 PROJECTED PRICE
SET	$8,500	$10,700	$5,300	1.5x	$16,000	$20,000
Konstanty	$2,000	$3,000	$1,500	1.5x	$4,500	$5,000
Roberts	$2,500	$3,000	$1,500	1.5x	$4,500	$5,000
Stanky	$2,500	$3,000	$1,500	1.5x	$4,500	$4,500
Berra	$450	$350	$175	1.5x	$525	$550
Rizzuto	$450	$300	$50	1.2x	$350	$350
Kiner	$350	$250	$75	1.3x	$325	$375
Lemon	$400	$250	$75	1.3x	$325	$375

continued

SET CHARTS

CARDS	1980 PRICE	1985 PRICE	$ INCREASE SINCE 1985	RATE INCREASE SINCE 1985	1988 PRICE	1989 PROJECTED PRICE
Kell	$225	$250	$50	1.2x	$300	$400
Doby	$450	$160	$65	1.4x	$225	$275
Dropo	$300	$180	$45	1.3x	$225	$275
Evers	$225	$120	$30	1.3x	$150	$150

See the note at the bottom of the previous chart.

TOPPS RED BACKS 1951
(52 CARDS/APPROX. 30 COMMONS)

CARDS	1980 PRICE	1985 PRICE	$ INCREASE SINCE 1985	RATE INCREASE SINCE 1985	1988 PRICE	1989 PROJECTED PRICE
SET	$175	$225	$275	2.2x	$500	$620
Berra	$15	$21	$29	2.4x	$50	$70
Snider	$13.50	$16	$24	2.5x	$40	$60

BOWMAN 1952
(252 CARDS/APPROX. 140 COMMONS)

CARDS	1980 PRICE	1985 PRICE	$ INCREASE SINCE 1985	RATE INCREASE SINCE 1985	1988 PRICE	1989 PROJECTED PRICE
SET	$825	$1,050	$4,950	5.7x	$6,000	$7,200
Mantle	$160	$220	$780	4.5x	$1,000	$1,200
Mays	$180	$180	$270	2.5x	$450	$650
Berra	$35	$50	$325	7.5x	$375	$425
Musial	$60	$70	$180	3.6x	$250	$300
Campanella	$23	$32	$68	3.1x	$100	$100

TOPPS 1952
(407 CARDS/APPROX. 285 COMMONS)

CARDS	1980 PRICE	1985 PRICE	$ INCREASE SINCE 1985	RATE INCREASE SINCE 1985	1988 PRICE	1989 PROJECTED PRICE
SET	$10,000	$9,600	$26,400	3.8x	$36,000	$38,000
Mantle	$2,500	$2,100	$4,400	3.1x	$6,500	$6,500
Mathews	$400	$400	$1,000	3.5x	$1,400	$1,800
Mays	$350	$325	$475	2.5x	$800	$875
Campanella	$350	$350	$425	2.2x	$775	$1,100
JRobinson	$375	$285	$225	2.1x	$600	$600
Pafko*	$15	$125	$425	4.4x	$550	$1,200

continued

SET CHARTS

CARDS	1980 PRICE	1985 PRICE	$ INCREASE SINCE 1985	RATE INCREASE SINCE 1985	1988 PRICE	1989 PROJECTED PRICE
Reese	$175	$225	$225	2x	$450	$550
Dickey	$350	$225	$225	2x	$450	$550
Wilhelm	$100	$165	$210	2.3x	$375	$425

*The No. 1 Pafko card in mint condition has been sold for as much as $16,000 in the last year, although the price guides have listed it at around $1,400; and the near-mint card at $1,000.

BOWMAN COLOR 1953
(160 CARDS/APPROX. 85 COMMONS)

CARDS	1980 PRICE	1985 PRICE	$ INCREASE SINCE 1985	RATE INCREASE SINCE 1985	1988 PRICE	1989 PROJECTED PRICE
SET	$1,400	$1,800	$4,200	3.3x	$6,000	$7,200
Mantle	$175	$220	$680	4.1x	$900	$1,500
Snider	$130	$150	$200	2.3x	$350	$400
Berra	$80	$125	$200	2.6x	$325	$475
Ford	$50	$60	$190	4.2x	$250	$350
Musial	$75	$85	$165	2.9x	$250	$250
Bauer, Berra, & Mantle	$50	$50	$200	5x	$250	$300
Martin	$30	$42	$108	3.6x	$150	$200

continued

GETTING SERIOUS

CARDS	1980 PRICE	1985 PRICE	$ INCREASE SINCE 1985	RATE INCREASE SINCE 1985	1988 PRICE	1989 PROJECTED PRICE
Feller	$55	$60	$90	2.5x	$150	$170
Campanella	$30	$42	$98	3.3x	$140	$160
Reese	$14	$25	$75	4x	$100	$200
Martin & Rizzuto	$25	$36	$64	2.8x	$100	$150

<u>BOWMAN B&W 1953</u>
(64 CARDS/APPROX. 40 COMMONS)

CARDS	1980 PRICE	1985 PRICE	$ INCREASE SINCE 1985	RATE INCREASE SINCE 1985	1988 PRICE	1989 PROJECTED PRICE
SET	$850	$800	$1,175	2.5x	$1,975	$2,400
Stengel	$120	$120	$105	1.9x	$225	$225

SET CHARTS

TOPPS 1953
(274 CARDS/APPROX. 150 COMMONS)

CARDS	1980 PRICE	1985 PRICE	$ INCREASE SINCE 1985	RATE INCREASE SINCE 1985	1988 PRICE	1989 PROJECTED PRICE
SET	$1,450	$1,800	$6,200	4.4x	$8,000	$9,000
Mantle	$150	$250	$950	4.8x	$1,200	$2,000
Mays	$500	$400	$450	2.1x	$850	$1,500
JRobinson	$35	$54	$246	5.6x	$300	$700
MBolling*	$12	$24	$176	8.3x	$200	$250
Paige	$28	$40	$160	5x	$200	$220
Podres	$12	$24	$151	7.3x	$175	$175
Gilliam	$20	$36	$139	4.9x	$175	$200
Campanella	$23	$32	$78	3.4x	$110	$140
Berra	$20	$30	$70	3.3x	$100	$120

*Milt Bolling is the last card of the set.

BOWMAN 1954
(224 CARDS/APPROX. 120 COMMONS)

CARDS	1980 PRICE	1985 PRICE	$ INCREASE SINCE 1985	RATE INCREASE SINCE 1985	1988 PRICE	1989 PROJECTED PRICE
SET	$775	$550	2,050	4.7x	$2,600	$3,300
TWilliams	$450	$650	$850	2.3x	$1,500	$1,700
Mantle	$65	$100	$425	5.3x	$525	$725
Mays	$60	$75	$100	2.33x	$175	$175

TOPPS 1954
(250 CARDS/APPROX. 165 COMMONS)

CARDS	1980 PRICE	1985 PRICE	$ INCREASE SINCE 1985	RATE INCREASE SINCE 1985	1988 PRICE	1989 PROJECTED PRICE
SET	$550	$820	$3,980	5.9x	$4,800	$5,800
Aaron	$185	$175	$325	2.9x	$500	$700
TWilliams No. 1	$35	$60	$265	5.4x	$325	$325
TWilliams No. 250	$32	$60	$265	5.4x	$325	$325
Banks	$30	$55	$245	5.5x	$300	$550
Kaline	$25	$65	$235	4.6x	$300	$550
Mays	$80	$90	$110	2.2x	$200	$200
Lasorda	$5	$6	$94	16.7x	$100	$120
Berra	$16	$25	$75	4x	$100	$120
JRobinson	$18	$32	$68	3.1x	$100	$150

BOWMAN 1955
(320 CARDS/APPROX. 185 COMMONS)

CARDS	1980 PRICE	1985 PRICE	$ INCREASE SINCE 1985	RATE INCREASE SINCE 1985	1988 PRICE	1989 PROJECTED PRICE
SET	$390	$550	$2,750	6x	$3,300	$3,600
Mantle	$30	$50	$250	6x	$300	$350
Banks	$42	$50	$150	4x	$200	$225
Aaron	$25	$35	$65	2.9x	$100	$120

SET CHARTS

TOPPS 1955
(206 CARDS/APPROX. 132 COMMONS)

CARDS	1980 PRICE	1985 PRICE	$ INCREASE SINCE 1985	RATE INCREASE SINCE 1985	1988 PRICE	1989 PROJECTED PRICE
SET	$500	$600	$2,900	5.8x	$3,500	$4,200
Clemente	$90	$100	$225	3.2x	$325	$525
Snider	$42	$100	$175	2.8x	$275	$325
Mays	$140	$140	$135	2x	$275	$325
Koufax	$25	$60	$190	4.2x	$250	$400
TWilliams	$25	$36	$114	4.2x	$150	$150
Berra	$32	$38	$87	3.3x	$125	$125
Aaron	$30	$40	$85	3.1x	$125	$175
Killebrew	$10	$26	$74	3.8x	$100	$220
Rizzuto	$18	$26	$74	3.8x	$100	$100
Hodges	$23	$30	$70	3.3x	$100	$100

TOPPS 1956
(340 CARDS/APPROX. 200 COMMONS)

CARDS	1980 PRICE	1985 PRICE	$ INCREASE SINCE 1985	RATE INCREASE SINCE 1985	1988 PRICE	1989 PROJECTED PRICE
SET (without two checklists)	$380	$640	$2,960	5.6x	$3,600	$4,200
Mantle	$40	$85	$415	5.9x	$500	$700

continued

187

GETTING SERIOUS

CARDS	1980 PRICE	1985 PRICE	$ INCREASE SINCE 1985	RATE INCREASE SINCE 1985	1988 PRICE	1989 PROJECTED PRICE
TWilliams	$20	$32	$93	3.9x	$125	$125
Checklist 1/3	—	$50	$75	2.5x	$125	$175
Checklist 2/4	—	$50	$75	2.5x	$125	$175
Koufax	$14	$28	$72	3.6x	$100	$120
Clemente	$20	$28	$72	3.6x	$100	$120
Mays	$28	$40	$60	2.5x	$100	$150

TOPPS 1957
(407–415 CARDS/APPROX. 235 COMMONS)

CARDS	1980 PRICE	1985 PRICE	$ INCREASE SINCE 1985	RATE INCREASE SINCE 1985	1988 PRICE	1989 PROJECTED PRICE
SET (without four checklists)	$525	$770	$3,730	5.8x	$4,500	$4,800
Mantle	$30	$75	$425	6.7x	$500	$700
TWilliams	$22	$45	$205	5.6x	$250	$350
Koufax	$70	$75	$125	2.7x	$200	$350
Checklist 4/5	—	$80	$120	2.5x	$200	$450
BRobinson	$70	$85	$115	2.4x	$200	$300

continued

SET CHARTS

CARDS	1980 PRICE	1985 PRICE	$ INCREASE SINCE 1985	RATE INCREASE SINCE 1985	1988 PRICE	1989 PROJECTED PRICE
Berra & Mantle	$10	$24	$151	7.3x	$175	$275
Checklist 3/4	—	$60	$90	2.5x	$150	$350
Dodger Sluggers	$7.50	$20	$80	5x	$100	$150
Checklist 2/3	—	$30	$70	3.3x	$100	$175
FRobinson	$10	$34	$66	2.9x	$100	$125
Mays	$23	$34	$66	2.9x	$100	$100
Aaron	$25	$40	$60	2.5x	$100	$100

TOPPS 1958
(494 CARDS/APPROX. 280 COMMONS)

CARDS	1980 PRICE	1985 PRICE	$ INCREASE SINCE 1985	RATE INCREASE SINCE 1985	1988 PRICE	1989 PROJECTED PRICE
SET	$320	$470	$2,330	6x	$2,800	$3,300
Mantle	$23	$50	$275	6.5x	$325	$475
Maris	$5	$20	$205	11.3x	$225	$275
TWilliams	$18	$45	$180	5x	$225	$275
Aaron	$20	$60	$40	1.7x	$100	$150

TOPPS 1959
(572 CARDS/APPROX. 350 COMMONS)

CARDS	1980 PRICE	1985 PRICE	$ INCREASE SINCE 1985	RATE INCREASE SINCE 1985	1988 PRICE	1989 PROJECTED PRICE
SET	$260	$440	$2,360	6.4x	$2,800	$3,100
Mantle	$16	$40	$235	6.9x	$275	$325
Gibson	$9	$28	$97	4.5x	$125	$275
Mantle AS	$12	$24	$76	4.2x	$100	$150

TOPPS 1960
(572 CARDS/APPROX. 335 COMMONS)

CARDS	1980 PRICE	1985 PRICE	$ INCREASE SINCE 1985	RATE INCREASE SINCE 1985	1988 PRICE	1989 PROJECTED PRICE
SET	$250	$430	$2,070	5.8x	$2,500	$3,000
Mantle	$14	$35	$240	7.9x	$275	$325
Yastrzemski	$12	$80	$70	1.9x	$150	$200
Mantle AS	$12	$24	$76	4.2x	$100	$150

SET CHARTS

TOPPS 1961
(587 CARDS/APPROX. 340 COMMONS)

CARDS	1980 PRICE	1985 PRICE	$ INCREASE SINCE 1985	RATE INCREASE SINCE 1985	1988 PRICE	1989 PROJECTED PRICE
SET	$525	$730	$2,870	4.9x	$3,600	$3,800
Mantle AS	$30	$75	$150	3x	$225	$225
Mantle	$13	$33	$167	6.1x	$200	$200
Aaron AS	$30	$45	$55	2.2x	$100	$100
Mays AS	$30	$45	$55	2.2x	$100	$100

TOPPS 1962
(598 CARDS/APPROX. 270 COMMONS)

CARDS	1980 PRICE	1985 PRICE	$ INCREASE SINCE 1985	RATE INCREASE SINCE 1985	1988 PRICE	1989 PROJECTED PRICE
SET	$260	$470	$2,730	6.8x	$3,200	$3,400
Mantle	$12	$32	$268	9.4x	$300	$350
Maris	$4.50	$16	$109	7.8x	$125	$175
Yastrzemski	$9	$48	$77	2.6x	$125	$150
Uecker	$2	$6	$84	15x	$90	$90

FLEER 1963
(67 CARDS/APPROX. 33 COMMONS)

CARDS	1980 PRICE	1985 PRICE	$ INCREASE SINCE 1985	RATE INCREASE SINCE 1985	1988 PRICE	1989 PROJECTED PRICE
SET (without checklist)	$75	$160	$240	2.5x	$400	$450
Checklist	$16	$40	$50	2.3x	$90	$200
Adcock	$21	$33	$21	1.6x	$54	$56

Joe Adcock's card was dropped halfway through the production run, and a checklist was inserted to replace it. As a result, both are rare (and if we were Joe, we'd resent the differential).

TOPPS 1963
(576 CARDS/APPROX. 265 COMMONS)

CARDS	1980 PRICE	1985 PRICE	$ INCREASE SINCE 1985	RATE INCREASE SINCE 1985	1988 PRICE	1989 PROJECTED PRICE
SET	$350	$760	$1,940	3.6x	$2,700	$3,300
Rose	$35	$300	$250	1.8x	$550	$550
Mantle	$17	$33	$217	7.6x	$250	$250
Stargell	$7	$33	$67	3x	$100	$150
Clemente	$35	$40	$60	2.5x	$100	$120

TOPPS 1964
(587 CARDS/APPROX. 300 COMMONS)

CARDS	1980 PRICE	1985 PRICE	$ INCREASE SINCE 1985	RATE INCREASE SINCE 1985	1988 PRICE	1989 PROJECTED PRICE
SET	$190	$400	$1,300	4.3x	$1,700	$1,900
Mantle	$10	$24	$151	7.3x	$175	$175
Rose	$10	$85	$45	1.5x	$130	$140

TOPPS 1965
(587 CARDS/APPROX. 287 COMMONS)

CARDS	1980 PRICE	1985 PRICE	$ INCREASE SINCE 1985	RATE INCREASE SINCE 1985	1988 PRICE	1989 PROJECTED PRICE
SET	$190	$450	$1,550	4.4x	$2,000	$2,200
Mantle	$9	$29	$296	11.2x	$325	$325
Rose	$8	$75	$65	1.9x	$140	$140
Carlton	$1.25	$100	$0	0x	$100	$120

TOPPS 1966
(598 CARDS/APPROX. 300 COMMONS)

CARDS	1980 PRICE	1985 PRICE	$ INCREASE SINCE 1985	RATE INCREASE SINCE 1985	1988 PRICE	1989 PROJECTED PRICE
SET	$260	$500	$1,700	4.4x	$2,200	$2,500
Mantle	$8.50	$23	$152	7.6x	$175	$175
GPerry	$10	$50	$100	3x	$150	$200
Mays	$7.50	$25	$75	4x	$100	$100

TOPPS 1967
(609 CARDS/APPROX. 310 COMMONS)

CARDS	1980 PRICE	1985 PRICE	$ INCREASE SINCE 1985	RATE INCREASE SINCE 1985	1988 PRICE	1989 PROJECTED PRICE
SET	$360	$700	$1,700	3.4x	$2,400	$2,600
Seaver	$45	$95	$305	4.2x	$400	$500
Mantle	$8	$24	$151	7.3x	$175	$175
Carew	$20	$75	$50	1.7x	$125	$125
BRobinson	$130	$85	$40	1.5x	$125	$125

SET CHARTS

TOPPS 1968
(598 CARDS/APPROX. 325 COMMONS)

CARDS	1980 PRICE	1985 PRICE	$ INCREASE SINCE 1985	RATE INCREASE SINCE 1985	1988 PRICE	1989 PROJECTED PRICE
SET	$140	$325	$975	4x	$1,300	$1,500
Mantle	$7	$20	$130	7.5x	$150	$150
Ryan	$4	$35	$90	3.6x	$125	$150
Bench	$5	$100	$25	1.3x	$125	$190

TOPPS 1969
(664 CARDS/APPROX. 300 COMMONS)

CARDS	1980 PRICE	1985 PRICE	$ INCREASE SINCE 1985	RATE INCREASE SINCE 1985	1988 PRICE	1989 PROJECTED PRICE
SET (without white-letter variations)	$130	$400	$850	3.1x	$1,250	$1,400
Mantle (white letters)	$8	$66	$284	5.3x	$350	$350
RJackson	$4	$60	$140	3.3x	$200	$220
Mantle (yellow letters)	$8	$24	$126	6.3x	$150	$150

TOPPS 1970*
(720 CARDS/APPROX. 400 COMMONS)

CARDS	1980 PRICE	1985 PRICE	$ INCREASE SINCE 1985	RATE INCREASE SINCE 1985	1988 PRICE	1989 PROJECTED PRICE
SET	$140	$360	$540	2.5x	$900	$1,100
Bench	$30	$42	$33	1.7x	$75	$90
Rose	$5	$31	$39	2.3x	$70	$80
Ryan	$6.50	$15	$25	2.7x	$40	$50
RJackson	$1.75	$13.50	$16.50	2.2x	$30	$50
Munson	$2	$15.50	$14.50	1.9x	$30	$40
Mays	$7	$12.50	$11.50	1.9x	$24	$32
Seaver	$3	$11	$9	1.8x	$20	$25

*Beginning with this set, we have listed only those individual cards that were priced at $20 or more in 1988.

TOPPS 1971
(752 CARDS/APPROX. 430 COMMONS)

CARDS	1980 PRICE	1985 PRICE	$ INCREASE SINCE 1985	RATE INCREASE SINCE 1985	1988 PRICE	1989 PROJECTED PRICE
SET	$115	$385	$615	2.6x	$1,000	$1,200
Garvey	$4	$28	$27	2x	$55	$65
Rose	$3	$21	$24	2.1x	$45	$55
Mays	$5	$13	$12	1.9x	$25	$32
Yastrzemski	$4.50	$12.50	$11.50	1.9x	$24	$31

continued

SET CHARTS

CARDS	1980 PRICE	1985 PRICE	$ INCREASE SINCE 1985	RATE INCREASE SINCE 1985	1988 PRICE	1989 PROJECTED PRICE
Clemente	$4.50	$9.50	$10.50	2.1x	$20	$25
RJackson	$1.75	$10	$10	2x	$20	$25
Baker-Baylor	$.50	$12.50	$7.50	1.6x	$20	$22

TOPPS 1972
(787 CARDS/APPROX. 420 COMMONS)

CARDS	1980 PRICE	1985 PRICE	$ INCREASE SINCE 1985	RATE INCREASE SINCE 1985	1988 PRICE	1989 PROJECTED PRICE
SET	$130	$380	$520	2.4x	$900	$1,100
Garvey	$10	$40	$25	1.6x	$65	$75
Carew No. 695	$16	$40	$20	1.5x	$60	$65
Rose No. 559	$3.25	$29	$26	1.9x	$55	$65
Carlton Traded	$1.50	$23	$7	1.3x	$30	$30
Rose No. 560	$1.75	$12.50	$12.50	2x	$25	$35
Carew No. 696	$8	$17	$8	1.5x	$25	$30

TOPPS 1973
(660 CARDS/APPROX. 240 COMMONS)

CARDS	1980 PRICE	1985 PRICE	$ INCREASE SINCE 1985	RATE INCREASE SINCE 1985	1988 PRICE	1989 PROJECTED PRICE
SET	$48	$225	$300	2.3x	$525	$650
Schmidt	$.65	$65	$85	2.3x	$150	$200
Rose	$1.75	$12	$8	1.7x	$20	$20

TOPPS 1974
(660 CARDS/APPROX. 240 COMMONS)

CARDS	1980 PRICE	1985 PRICE	$ INCREASE SINCE 1985	RATE INCREASE SINCE 1985	1988 PRICE	1989 PROJECTED PRICE
SET	$32	$180	$170	1.9x	$350	$450
Schmidt	$.25	$10	$25	3.5x	$35	$45
Winfield	$.65	$14	$11	1.8x	$25	$40
McCovey (Washington)	$2.50	$10	$10	2x	$20	$20

TOPPS TRADED 1974
(44 CARDS/APPROX. 30 COMMONS)

CARDS	1980 PRICE	1985 PRICE	$ INCREASE SINCE 1985	RATE INCREASE SINCE 1985	1988 PRICE	1989 PROJECTED PRICE
SET	$2.25	$5	$2	1.4x	$7	$8
Highest-Priced Card	$.06	$.90	$.35	1.4x	$1.25	$1.25

TOPPS 1975
(660 CARDS/APPROX. 340 COMMONS)

CARDS	1980 PRICE	1985 PRICE	$ INCREASE SINCE 1985	RATE INCREASE SINCE 1985	1988 PRICE	1989 PROJECTED PRICE
SET	$27	$210	$290	2.4x	$500	$600
GBrett	$.60	$20	$30	2.5x	$50	$50
Carter	$.05	$11	$29	3.6x	$40	$50
Rice	$1.25	$18	$22	2.2x	$40	$30
Yount	$.08	$16.50	$13.50	1.8x	$30	$30
Hernandez	$.30	$9	$16	2.8x	$25	$25

GETTING SERIOUS

TOPPS MINIS 1975
(660 CARDS/APPROX. 420 COMMONS)

CARDS	1980 PRICE	1985 PRICE	$ INCREASE SINCE 1985	RATE INCREASE SINCE 1985	1988 PRICE	1989 PROJECTED PRICE
SET	$45	$210	$590	3.8x	$800	$1,000
GBrett	$.90	$40	$25	1.6x	$65	$65
Carter	$.07	$22	$38	2.7x	$60	$70
Rice	$1.87	$36	$24	1.7x	$60	$50
Schmidt	$.30	$17	$33	2.9x	$50	$50
Yount	$12	$33	$12	1.4x	$45	$45
Rose	$1.20	$20	$20	2x	$40	$40
Hernandez	$.45	$18	$17	1.9x	$35	$35
Aaron	$1.87	$13	$7	1.5x	$20	$20
RJackson	$.75	$8.50	$3.50	1.4x	$12	$14

TOPPS 1976
(660 CARDS/APPROX. 340 COMMONS)

CARDS	1980 PRICE	1985 PRICE	$ INCREASE SINCE 1985	RATE INCREASE SINCE 1985	1988 PRICE	1989 PROJECTED PRICE
SET	$21	$120	$130	2.1x	$250	$330
Highest-Priced Card	$1.25	$8	$7	1.9x	$15	$15

SET CHARTS

TOPPS TRADED 1976
(44 CARDS/APPROX. 25 COMMONS)

CARDS	1980 PRICE	1985 PRICE	$ INCREASE SINCE 1985	RATE INCREASE SINCE 1985	1988 PRICE	1989 PROJECTED PRICE
SET	$2	$5	$3	1.6x	$8	$10
Highest-Priced Card	$.40	$.35	$.45	2.3x	$.80	$.90

TOPPS 1977
(660 CARDS/APPROX. 340 COMMONS)

CARDS	1980 PRICE	1985 PRICE	$ INCREASE SINCE 1985	RATE INCREASE SINCE 1985	1988 PRICE	1989 PROJECTED PRICE
SET	$19	$120	$130	2.1x	$250	$330
Murphy	$.03	$27	$38	2.4x	$65	$65

TOPPS 1978
(726 CARDS/APPROX. 475 COMMONS)

CARDS	1980 PRICE	1985 PRICE	$ INCREASE SINCE 1985	RATE INCREASE SINCE 1985	1988 PRICE	1989 PROJECTED PRICE
SET	$16.50	$70	$130	2.9x	$200	$265
Murray	$.08	$16	$19	2.2x	$35	$40
Murphy & Parrish	$.03	$10.50	$19.50	2.9x	$30	$30
Molitor & Trammell	$.03	$7	$21	4x	$28	$35

TOPPS 1979
(726 CARDS/APPROX. 440 COMMONS)

CARDS	1980 PRICE	1985 PRICE	$ INCREASE SINCE 1985	RATE INCREASE SINCE 1985	1988 PRICE	1989 PROJECTED PRICE
SET	$15.50	$56	$79	2.4x	$135	$165
Highest-Priced Card	$1	$4.50	$3.50	1.8x	$8	$14

SET CHARTS

TOPPS 1980
(726 CARDS/APPROX. 500 COMMONS)

CARDS	1980 PRICE	1985 PRICE	$ INCREASE SINCE 1985	RATE INCREASE SINCE 1985	1988 PRICE	1989 PROJECTED PRICE
SET	$14	$45	$90	3x	$135	$165
RHenderson	$.03	$6.50	$21.50	4.3x	$28	$32

DONRUSS 1981
(605 CARDS/APPROX. 280 COMMONS)

CARDS	1980 PRICE	1985 PRICE	$ INCREASE SINCE 1985	RATE INCREASE SINCE 1985	1988 PRICE	1989 PROJECTED PRICE
SET	—	$21	$1	1.05x	$22	$22
Highest-Priced Card	—	$1.50	$3.50	3.3x	$5	$5

FLEER 1981
(660 CARDS/APPROX. 380 COMMONS)

CARDS	1980 PRICE	1985 PRICE	$ INCREASE SINCE 1985	RATE INCREASE SINCE 1985	1988 PRICE	1989 PROJECTED PRICE
SET	—	$21	−$1	.95x	$20	$20
Highest-Priced Card	—	$10	$2	1.2x	$12	$12

TOPPS 1981
(726 CARDS/APPROX. 440 COMMONS)

CARDS	1980 PRICE	1985 PRICE	$ INCREASE SINCE 1985	RATE INCREASE SINCE 1985	1988 PRICE	1989 PROJECTED PRICE
SET	—	$35	$45	2.3x	$80	$90
Highest-Priced Card	—	$6	$2.50	2.4x	$8.50	$9

TOPPS TRADED 1981
(132 CARDS/APPROX. 82 COMMONS)

CARDS	1980 PRICE	1985 PRICE	$ INCREASE SINCE 1985	RATE INCREASE SINCE 1985	1988 PRICE	1989 PROJECTED PRICE
SET	—	$16.50	$3.50	1.2x	$20	$22
Highest-Priced Card	—	$3	$3	2x	$6	$6

DONRUSS 1982
(660 CARDS/APPROX. 380 COMMONS)

CARDS	1980 PRICE	1985 PRICE	$ INCREASE SINCE 1985	RATE INCREASE SINCE 1985	1988 PRICE	1989 PROJECTED PRICE
SET	—	$16	$4	1.3x	$20	$20
Highest-Priced Card	—	$3.25	$4.75	2.5x	$8	$8

SET CHARTS

FLEER 1982
(660 CARDS/APPROX. 410 COMMONS)

CARDS	1980 PRICE	1985 PRICE	$ INCREASE SINCE 1985	RATE INCREASE SINCE 1985	1988 PRICE	1989 PROJECTED PRICE
SET (without variations)	—	$16	$4	1.3x	$20	$20
Littlefield variation	—	$36	$34	1.9x	$70	$70
Hrabosky variation	—	$10	$8	1.8x	$18	$18
Highest-Priced Card	—	$3.25	$4.75	2.5x	$8	$8

TOPPS 1982
(792 CARDS/APPROX. 400 COMMONS)

CARDS	1980 PRICE	1985 PRICE	$ INCREASE SINCE 1985	RATE INCREASE SINCE 1985	1988 PRICE	1989 PROJECTED PRICE
SET	—	$29	$46	2.6x	$75	$85
PPerez variation	—	$.10	$34.90	350x	$35	$35
Highest-Priced Card	—	$5.50	$6.50	2.2x	$12	$14

TOPPS TRADED 1982
(132 CARDS/APPROX. 71 COMMONS)

CARDS	1980 PRICE	1985 PRICE	$ INCREASE SINCE 1985	RATE INCREASE SINCE 1985	1988 PRICE	1989 PROJECTED PRICE
SET	—	$12.50	$7.50	1.6x	$20	$22
Highest-Priced Card	—	$4.25	$3.25	1.8x	$7.50	$7.50

DONRUSS 1983
(660 CARDS/APPROX. 350 COMMONS)

CARDS	1980 PRICE	1985 PRICE	$ INCREASE SINCE 1985	RATE INCREASE SINCE 1985	1988 PRICE	1989 PROJECTED PRICE
SET	—	$15	$13	1.9x	$28	$30
Highest-Priced Card	—	$2.25	$14.75	7.6x	$17	$19

FLEER 1983
(660 CARDS/APPROX. 410 COMMONS)

CARDS	1980 PRICE	1985 PRICE	$ INCREASE SINCE 1985	RATE INCREASE SINCE 1985	1988 PRICE	1989 PROJECTED PRICE
SET	—	$15	$19	2.3x	$34	$37
Highest-Priced Card	—	$2.25	$14.75	7.6x	$17	$19

SET CHARTS

TOPPS 1983
(792 CARDS/approx. 400 COMMONS)

CARDS	1980 PRICE	1985 PRICE	$ INCREASE SINCE 1985	RATE INCREASE SINCE 1985	1988 PRICE	1989 PROJECTED PRICE
SET	—	$25	$55	3.2x	$80	$90
Boggs	—	$3.75	$26.25	8x	$30	$34

TOPPS TRADED 1983
(132 CARDS/APPROX. 80 COMMONS)

CARDS	1980 PRICE	1985 PRICE	$ INCREASE SINCE 1985	RATE INCREASE SINCE 1985	1988 PRICE	1989 PROJECTED PRICE
SET	—	$12.50	$25.50	3x	$38	$40
Strawberry	—	$4	$20	6x	$24	$30

DONRUSS 1984
(660 CARDS/APPROX. 330 COMMONS)

CARDS	1980 PRICE	1985 PRICE	$ INCREASE SINCE 1985	RATE INCREASE SINCE 1985	1988 PRICE	1989 PROJECTED PRICE
SET	—	$23	$177	8.7x	$200	$250
Mattingly	—	$3.25	$61.75	20x	$65	$65

FLEER 1984
(660 CARDS/APPROX. 375 COMMONS)

CARDS	1980 PRICE	1985 PRICE	$ INCREASE SINCE 1985	RATE INCREASE SINCE 1985	1988 PRICE	1989 PROJECTED PRICE
SET	—	$14	$61	5.4x	$75	$85
Mattingly	—	$2.25	$27.25	13.3x	$30	$27

FLEER UPDATE 1984
(132 CARDS/APPROX. 65 COMMONS)

CARDS	1980 PRICE	1985 PRICE	$ INCREASE SINCE 1985	RATE INCREASE SINCE 1985	1988 PRICE	1989 PROJECTED PRICE
SET	—	$22	$203	10.2x	$225	$250
Clemens	—	$.50	$74.50	150x	$75	$75
Gooden	—	$5.50	$59.50	11.8x	$65	$75
Puckett	—	$1	$59	60x	$60	$65
Rose	—	$2	$23	12.5x	$25	$25
Saberhagen	—	$.30	$19.70	66.7x	$20	$20

SET CHARTS

TOPPS 1984
(792 CARDS/APPROX. 400 COMMONS)

CARDS	1980 PRICE	1985 PRICE	$ INCREASE SINCE 1985	RATE INCREASE SINCE 1985	1988 PRICE	1989 PROJECTED PRICE
SET	—	$21	$54	3.6x	$75	$85
Mattingly	—	$4.45	$22.55	6.1x	$27	$27

TOPPS TRADED 1984
(132 CARDS/APPROX. 66 COMMONS)

CARDS	1980 PRICE	1985 PRICE	$ INCREASE SINCE 1985	RATE INCREASE SINCE 1985	1988 PRICE	1989 PROJECTED PRICE
SET	—	$11	$64	6.8x	$75	$85
Gooden	—	$4.50	$30.50	7.8x	$35	$45

DONRUSS 1985
(660 CARDS/APPROX. 360 COMMONS)

CARDS	1980 PRICE	1985 PRICE	$ INCREASE SINCE 1985	RATE INCREASE SINCE 1985	1988 PRICE	1989 PROJECTED PRICE
SET	—	$17	$103	7.1x	$120	$140
EDavis	—	$.30	$24.70	83.3x	$25	$21

FLEER 1985
(660 COMMONS)

CARDS	1980 PRICE	1985 PRICE	$ INCREASE SINCE 1985	RATE INCREASE SINCE 1985	1988 PRICE	1989 PROJECTED PRICE
SET	—	$13	$62	5.8x	$75	$85
Highest-Priced Card	—	$2	$15	8.5x	$17	$17

FLEER UPDATE 1985
(132 CARDS/APPROX. 56 COMMONS)

CARDS	1980 PRICE	1985 PRICE	$ INCREASE SINCE 1985	RATE INCREASE SINCE 1985	1988 PRICE	1989 PROJECTED PRICE
SET	—	—	—	—	$16	$18
Highest-Priced Card	—	—	—	—	$4	$4

TOPPS 1985
(792 CARDS/APPROX. 450 COMMONS)

CARDS	1980 PRICE	1985 PRICE	$ INCREASE SINCE 1985	RATE INCREASE SINCE 1985	1988 PRICE	1989 PROJECTED PRICE
SET	—	$17	$73	5.3x	$90	$100
Highest-Priced Card	—	$3	$14	5.7x	$17	$17

TOPPS TRADED 1985
(132 CARDS/APPROX. 66 COMMONS)

CARDS	1980 PRICE	1985 PRICE	$ INCREASE SINCE 1985	RATE INCREASE SINCE 1985	1988 PRICE	1989 PROJECTED PRICE
SET	—	—	—	—	$14	$16
Highest-Priced Card	—	—	—	—	$4	$4

INDEX

ABOUT THE AUTHORS

BRUCE CHADWICK is a baseball card and entertainment columnist for the New York *Daily News* and frequently contributes to national magazines. A Syracuse University graduate, he lives in New Jersey with his wife Marjorie, an educator, and son Rory, 12, whose card collecting was the inspiration for his father's baseball card column.

DANNY PEARY was the sports Editor of *L.A. Panorama* and is the author of the annual *365 Sports-Facts-A-Year Calendar*. His wife Suzanne is a book editor and their daughter, Zoë, is majoring in microbiology at the University of Michigan. He asks that whoever stole his baseball card collection in the early seventies please return it.